Beyond GPT

Smarter AI for Small Business Marketing

Leveraging AI Agents, Like Manus That Think, Plan, and Execute

First edition

BEYOND GPT
Smarter AI for Small Business Marketing

By Elena Saris

CeolWaves

2025

UNITED STATES OF AMERICA

Table of Contents

INTRODUCTION

Navigating the New Frontier of Marketing

In today's hyper-competitive business landscape, small business owners often find themselves navigating a complex and ever-evolving marketing maze. The challenges are numerous and significant: limited budgets that demand every dollar be stretched to its maximum potential, severe time constraints that pull entrepreneurs in countless directions, a frequent lack of specialized marketing skills within small teams, and the relentless pressure to keep pace with rapidly changing digital trends and consumer behaviors. It can feel like an uphill battle, where the resources and expertise of larger corporations create an uneven playing field. However, a transformative shift is underway, driven by advancements in artificial intelligence (AI), offering unprecedented opportunities for small businesses to not only compete but to thrive.

Over the past year, tools like ChatGPT have reshaped how millions of people think about productivity and communication. These generative AI platforms have introduced a new way to create content, generate ideas, and save time — especially for small businesses. But while GPT-based tools are brilliant at producing responses and simulating conversation, they are inherently reactive. They wait for a prompt. **AI Agents, by**

contrast, are proactive. They don't just answer questions — they think ahead, plan campaigns, execute steps, and keep going even when you're not watching. This book explores how Ai Agents like Manus start where GPT stops: it's not simply a chatbot or a content generator, but a tireless strategist and doer designed for the realities of modern small business marketing.

That doesn't mean GPT is obsolete — far from it. You'll likely find yourself using both tools in tandem: GPT for quick, single-turn tasks like drafting a caption or generating a simple image, and Manus for multi-step projects and sustained strategic execution. While Manus does generate images other tools are currently more advanced in image generation like GPT-4 or DALL·E. Manus excels at orchestrating the creative process. It can help plan, prompt, and manage the creative process around them. It might write image prompts, coordinate asset requests, or ensure your visuals align with your broader strategy.

Artificial intelligence is no longer a futuristic concept confined to science fiction or the domain of tech giants. It has emerged as a powerful, accessible, and game-changing force capable of leveling the playing field for small and medium-sized businesses (SMBs) across all industries. AI-powered tools and agents are democratizing access to sophisticated marketing capabilities that were once out of reach for those with modest resources. This book is your comprehensive guide to understanding and harnessing advanced Agents – using Manus as the main example– to revolutionize your marketing efforts, achieve remarkable results, and unlock new avenues for growth. These same concepts will apply as new AI Agents become available. We will refer to Manus throughout the book as a leading example, but the strategies are universal.

Imagine having a dedicated, intelligent partner capable of assisting you with a vast array of marketing tasks. Think of an entity that can conduct in-depth market research, help you deeply understand your ideal customers, brainstorm innovative campaign ideas, draft compelling content for your website and social media, assist in optimizing your online presence, and even help streamline your workflows.

This is the potential that an Agent like Manus brings to your fingertips. It is designed to be more than just a tool; it functions as a versatile collaborator, a tireless researcher, and an efficient assistant, augmenting your capabilities and empowering you to achieve your marketing objectives with greater precision and efficiency.

This book is structured to provide you with a clear roadmap to mastering the art and science of leveraging an Agent for your small business marketing. We begin with understanding the core principles of AI in marketing and the specific functionalities that make an agent like Manus invaluable. From there, we will explore practical, actionable strategies for applying these capabilities across the entire marketing spectrum – from foundational market research and customer avatar development to crafting compelling content, building a robust online presence, and implementing effective campaigns. Each chapter is designed to equip you with the knowledge, techniques, and confidence to integrate AI seamlessly into your marketing operations.

It is crucial, however, to approach this journey with realistic expectations. While Agents offer extraordinary potential, they are most effective when viewed as partners in a human-AI collaboration. They are here to enhance human ingenuity, automate repetitive tasks, and provide data-driven insights, but they do not replace the strategic thinking, ethical judgment, and personal touch that you, the business owner, bring to your brand. This book will emphasize this collaborative synergy, showing you how to guide and direct your Agent to achieve optimal outcomes while maintaining full control over your brand's voice and strategic direction.

Ultimately, this guide is a message of empowerment. The marketing landscape may be complex, but with the right knowledge and tools, you can navigate it with confidence and creativity. By learning to master an Agent like Manus, you are not just adopting new technology; you are taking a significant step towards taking control of your marketing destiny, saving precious time and resources, and building a more resilient, competitive, and successful small business. AI Agents can transform your marketing from a source of stress into a powerful engine for growth and innovation.

Note: This book was created mainly with the help of Manus AI, a tool I trained and directed to reflect my thoughts, expertise, and intent. I strategically combined multiple AI platforms (including ChatGPT, Perplexity, NotebookLM, Gemini and Flowith) to ensure comprehensive accuracy and cross-verification of all content—the result reflects my own expertise and strategic thinking, while the process itself serves as a real-world example of what's possible when human insight meets AI efficiency.

CHAPTER 1

Understanding Your AI Marketing Agent – Core Capabilities and How It Works for You

To effectively leverage any powerful resource, a foundational understanding of its capabilities and operational principles is essential. This chapter demystifies the concept of an advanced Agent, specifically one designed to assist with marketing, providing a clear, non-technical overview of its core functionalities. The goal is to equip you, the small business owner, with the insight needed to confidently collaborate with such an agent, transforming it from a black box of technology into a transparent and indispensable partner in your marketing endeavors.

Deconstructing Your AI Agent: What Makes It Tick?

At its heart, an AI marketing agent is a sophisticated software program engineered to perform a range of tasks traditionally handled by human marketers. It operates based on complex algorithms, machine learning models, and vast datasets, enabling it to understand natural language, process information, generate creative content, and even assist with certain technical operations. Think of it not as a sentient being, but as an incredibly advanced assistant that has been trained extensively in the domain of marketing. It learns from the instructions it receives and the data it processes, continuously refining its ability to deliver relevant and useful outputs. The key to a successful partnership lies in clear communication and providing the right context for the tasks you assign.

Your AI Agent's Superpowers for Marketers: A Closer Look

An AI marketing agent comes equipped with a suite of capabilities that can be directly applied to enhance your marketing efforts. Understanding these "superpowers" will help you identify the myriad ways it can support your business:

- **Information Gathering & Fact-Checking: Your 24/7 Research Assistant** One of the most significant advantages is the ability to rapidly gather and synthesize information from a vast range of online sources. Whether you need to understand market trends, research competitors, find industry statistics, or verify specific facts, your Agent can scan, process, and summarize relevant data far more quickly than manual methods would allow. This capability turns hours of research into minutes, providing you with the foundational knowledge needed for informed decision-making.
- **Data Processing & Analysis: Turning Raw Data into Actionable Insights** Small businesses often collect data from various sources – website analytics, customer feedback, sales figures – but may lack the resources to analyze it effectively. An Agent can assist in processing this data (when provided in a suitable

format), identifying patterns, trends, and correlations that might otherwise go unnoticed. This can help you understand customer behavior better, measure campaign effectiveness, and identify areas for improvement, transforming raw numbers into strategic insights.

- **Versatile Content Creation: From Blog Posts and Emails to Ad Copy and Video Scripts** Creating engaging and consistent content is a cornerstone of modern marketing, but it is also incredibly time-consuming. Your Agent can be a prolific content creation partner, capable of drafting a wide array of marketing materials. This includes blog posts, articles, website copy, email newsletters, social media updates, compelling advertising copy, and even scripts for videos or podcasts. While human oversight and refinement are crucial to ensure brand alignment and quality, the agent can significantly accelerate the initial drafting process, overcoming writer's block and providing a solid foundation to build upon.
- **Coding & Development Assistance: Helping Build and Maintain Digital Assets** While not a replacement for skilled web developers, an Agent with coding capabilities can provide valuable assistance with simpler technical tasks. This might involve generating basic HTML/CSS structures for web pages, explaining code snippets, helping to debug minor issues, or offering advice on choosing appropriate website platforms or tools. For small businesses looking to manage their digital assets more effectively without a large technical team, this can be a significant boon.

- **Automation of Repetitive Processes: Freeing Up Your Valuable Time for Strategy** Many marketing workflows involve repetitive, time-intensive tasks such as data entry, content formatting, or generating routine reports. An Agent can help conceptualize how these processes can be streamlined or, in some cases, assist in automating parts of them. By offloading these tasks, you and your team can free up valuable time and mental energy to focus on higher-level strategic thinking, customer engagement, and business development.
- **Creative Ideation & Brainstorming: Your Partner for Innovative Marketing Ideas** Sometimes, the biggest challenge is coming up with fresh, creative ideas. An Agent can serve as an excellent brainstorming partner. It can generate diverse marketing campaign concepts, suggest unique angles for your content, help you explore different value propositions, or even propose unconventional solutions to marketing challenges. By providing a wide range of initial ideas, it can spark your own creativity and help you break out of conventional thinking patterns.

How Your AI Agent Learns and Adapts Through Interaction

It is important to understand that your Agent is not static; it is designed to learn and adapt, primarily through its interactions with you. The more clearly you define your requirements, provide context, and offer feedback on its outputs, the better it becomes at understanding your specific needs, brand voice, and preferred style. This iterative process is key. If an initial output isn't perfect, refining your instructions or providing examples of what you're looking for will help the agent adjust and improve its subsequent responses. Think of it as training an assistant – clear guidance leads to better performance over time.

The Interface: Navigating and Communicating Effectively

Communicating with your Agent typically occurs through a text-based interface, where you provide instructions (often called "prompts") and receive responses. Effective communication hinges on clarity and specificity. Vague or ambiguous instructions are likely to yield generic or unhelpful results. The more detailed and well-structured your prompts are, the more accurately the agent can interpret your intent and deliver the desired outcome. Later chapters will explore the art of crafting effective prompts, a critical skill for maximizing the agent's utility.

The Crucial Role of Clear Instructions: An Introduction to Effective Prompting

As mentioned, the quality of your instructions directly impacts the quality of the Agent's output. Effective prompting involves more than just asking a question; it's about providing sufficient context, defining the desired format and tone, specifying constraints, and clearly stating the objective of the task. For instance, instead of asking for "marketing ideas," a more effective prompt would be, "Generate five unique marketing campaign ideas for a small independent bookstore targeting young adults, with a focus on community engagement and a budget under $500." This level of detail guides the agent towards a much more relevant and actionable response.

Understanding the Differences Between Prompts for GPT and Prompts for Manus

Prompt for GPT:

"Write a social media post for a local bookstore promoting a new event for young adult readers. Make it friendly and engaging. Limit to 150 words."

GPT will respond with a one-time output — often a well-written post — but it won't retain context or take initiative beyond that prompt.

Prompt for Manus:

"Help me build a complete campaign to promote a new weekly event for young adult readers at my local bookstore. The campaign should include social posts, email copy, a landing page draft, and a rollout calendar for the next 30 days. Stay under a $500 budget and make community engagement the central theme. Let's start with a brief plan."

Manus will begin by mapping out the components, asking clarifying questions if needed, and then progressively building and refining each element. It will track progress, reuse context across tasks, and help you manage execution — not just give you a single answer.

This difference is fundamental. **GPT responds. Manus collaborates.** That shift in power means your prompts can be broader and more strategic — you're not giving one command: you're giving collaborative directions.

Collaboration is Key: Working *With* Your Agent, Not Just Delegating Tasks

To truly master the use of an AI marketing agent, shift your mindset from mere delegation to active collaboration. View the agent as an extension of your team, a powerful assistant that requires your guidance, strategic input, and critical evaluation. Use its outputs as a starting point, a source of inspiration, or a first draft that you then refine, personalize, and infuse with your unique brand identity and human insight. The most successful applications of AI in marketing come from this synergistic partnership between human intelligence and artificial capability.

Ethical Considerations: Using AI Responsibly and Transparently

As with any powerful technology, the use of AI in marketing comes with ethical responsibilities. It is crucial to be transparent about the use of AI-generated content where appropriate, to ensure the accuracy of information, to respect data privacy and copyright, and to avoid perpetuating biases that may be present in training data. Responsible AI use builds trust with your audience and aligns with good business practices. This book will touch upon these considerations, encouraging an ethical approach to integrating AI into your marketing strategies.

By understanding these core capabilities and principles, you are now better prepared to explore the specific applications of an AI marketing agent across various facets of your small business marketing, which the subsequent chapters will detail with practical examples and actionable strategies.

Pro Tip: You don't have to figure it all out on your own — Manus can teach you how to use Manus. Simply ask, *"How should I prompt you for this?"* or *"Walk me through how you would approach this task step by step."* It will explain its capabilities, ask clarifying questions, and even help you refine your prompts, so you get better results.

CHAPTER 2

Knowledge Bases and Specialized AI Approaches for Small Business Marketing

In Chapter 1, we explored the core capabilities of AI marketing agents and how they can assist with various aspects of your small business marketing. Before examining specific marketing applications like market research and customer avatar development, it is important to understand two powerful concepts that can significantly enhance your results: knowledge bases and specialized AI approaches.

[A Note To Newer AI Users: If this chapter seems confusing, do not fear. Knowledge bases are optional and just a way of organizing your outputs for future use. You can skip to Chapter 3 and come back to this chapter after you understand what is possible and why you would want it organized and retrievable for future prompts]

These concepts represent more advanced approaches to working with AI, but they are increasingly accessible to small businesses and can provide substantial advantages in your marketing efforts. This chapter introduces these concepts and provides step-by-step instructions for implementation.

Understanding Knowledge Bases

A knowledge base is essentially a structured collection of information specific to your business that your AI marketing agent can reference when assisting you. Think of it as your business's institutional memory—a centralized repository of your products, services, brand voice, customer insights, and marketing history.

Unlike the general knowledge that AI systems possess from their training, a knowledge base contains your specific business information. This distinction is crucial because it allows the AI to provide responses that are accurate, relevant, and aligned with your unique business context rather than generic advice.

For small business owners, knowledge bases offer several key benefits

Consistency: Every interaction with your AI agent draws from the same source of truth, ensuring consistent messaging and recommendations across all your marketing efforts.

Efficiency: Rather than repeatedly explaining your business details, product specifications, or brand guidelines, you can reference your knowledge base and build upon previous work.

Personalization: Your AI agent can provide more tailored marketing assistance when it has access to your specific customer segments, past campaign performance, and business objectives.

Institutional Memory: As your business evolves, your knowledge base preserves insights, successful approaches, and lessons learned, creating a valuable asset that grows over time.

Creating Knowledge Bases in Manus

Creating knowledge bases in Manus requires no technical expertise. Follow these specific steps:

1. Access the Knowledge feature:

- Log into your Manus account
- Click on your account name located at the bottom left corner of the interface
- In the menu that appears, select "Knowledge"

2. Create a new Knowledge entry:

- On the Knowledge management screen, locate and click the "Add knowledge" button in the top right corner
- This will open the "Add Knowledge" dialog

3. Configure your Knowledge entry:

- In the "Name" field, enter a descriptive name for this knowledge (e.g., "Brand Guidelines" or "Customer Personas")
- In the "Manus will uses this knowledge when..." field, describe the specific situations when this knowledge should be applied
- In the "Content" field, enter or paste the actual information you want Manus to know
- Ensure the "Enabled" toggle is switched on
- Click "Save" to create your knowledge entry

4. Manage your Knowledge entries:

- All your knowledge entries will appear on the Knowledge management screen

- Each entry shows its name, content preview, creation date, and status
- You can enable/disable entries using the toggle switch
- You can edit or delete entries using the options provided for each entry
- The interface supports up to 50 knowledge entries

5. Reference your Knowledge in conversations:

- When starting a new conversation with Manus, your enabled knowledge entries will be automatically available
- You can explicitly reference specific knowledge by name in your prompts
- Manus will use this information to provide more relevant and personalized responses

Once your knowledge entries are set up, you do not need to re-upload or copy-paste this information for each conversation. Manus maintains access to your enabled knowledge entries and can reference them when responding to your prompts.

Essential Knowledge Base Categories for Marketing

While you will develop your own organizational system based on your business needs, here are some essential categories to consider for your marketing knowledge base:

Customer and Audience Information

- Detailed customer personas and segments
- Common questions, objections, and pain points
- Customer testimonials and feedback

- Audience demographics and psychographics

Product and Service Details

- Complete product/service descriptions
- Pricing structures and options
- Unique selling propositions
- Frequently asked questions and answers

Brand Voice and Messaging

- Brand personality and tone guidelines
- Key messaging frameworks and value propositions
- Approved language and terminology
- Phrases or approaches to avoid

Campaign History and Performance

- Past campaign objectives and strategies
- Performance metrics and results
- Creative assets and messaging used
- Lessons learned and insights gained

Research Findings

- Competitor analysis and positioning
- Market trends and opportunities
- Industry benchmarks and standards
- Customer research insights

Content Templates and Snippets

- Email templates for different purposes
- Social media post frameworks
- Blog post structures
- Ad copy formulas that work for your audience

As you progress through this book, you will encounter numerous prompts and techniques for various marketing tasks. While we will not explicitly instruct you to add each insight to your knowledge base, we strongly encourage you to develop the habit of documenting valuable outputs, successful prompts, and effective approaches. This documentation will become an increasingly valuable resource that enhances all your future marketing efforts.

Integrating Knowledge Bases Throughout Your Marketing

The true power of knowledge bases emerges when you consistently reference them in your AI interactions. Here are some practical ways to integrate your knowledge base into your marketing workflows:

When conducting market research (Chapter 3), reference your competitor knowledge to ensure your AI agent has accurate information about your competitive landscape.

When developing customer avatars (Chapter 4), build upon your existing customer insights rather than starting from scratch each time.

When creating content (Chapter 11), provide your brand voice guidelines and successful past examples to ensure consistency and effectiveness.

When analyzing campaign performance, compare current results against your historical data to identify meaningful patterns and improvements.

Here is an example of how to reference your knowledge base in a prompt:

"I'm working on a new email campaign for our premium skincare line. Please reference our brand voice guidelines that I've added to our knowledge base named [name of knowledge base]. Based on our previous email campaign performance metrics that I've also included in the knowledge base, help me draft an email announcement for our new anti-aging serum that's consistent with our brand voice and incorporates what we've learned from our previous campaigns."

By explicitly directing Manus to reference your knowledge base, you provide crucial context that helps your AI agent deliver more relevant, personalized, and effective assistance.

Understanding Specialized AI Approaches

Beyond knowledge bases, another powerful approach is developing specialized AI approaches for different marketing functions. Rather than using a single, general-purpose approach for all your marketing tasks, you can create specialized approaches that are optimized for specific types of work.

A specialized AI approach is not a separate system—it is a particular way of working with Manus that includes:

1. **Specific instructions** tailored to a particular marketing function

2. **Relevant examples** that demonstrate your preferred approach

3. **Evaluation criteria** for assessing outputs in that domain

4. **Reference to function-specific knowledge**

Specialized AI approaches offer several advantages over general-purpose approaches:

Improved quality: By focusing on a specific function, you can provide more detailed guidance and examples, resulting in better outputs.

Consistent methodology: Each specialized approach follows a consistent pattern for its particular function, creating more reliable results.

Efficient interactions: With established parameters and expectations, you spend less time explaining and more time accomplishing your marketing objectives.

Function-specific learning: Over time, you refine each specialized approach based on what works best for that particular marketing function.

Creating Specialized AI Approaches

While Manus does not have a dedicated "Agents" feature (yet!), you can create specialized approaches through consistent prompting patterns. Here's how to develop specialized approaches for different marketing functions:

1. Define the function's purpose:

- Clearly identify what specific marketing task this approach will address
- Document the exact outcomes you want to achieve

2. Create a standard prompt template:

- Write a detailed prompt that specifies the role, task, and expectations

- Include specific instructions about format, tone, and methodology
- Reference relevant knowledge entries that should inform this function

3. Save your specialized prompt templates:

- Store these templates in a document for easy reference
- Consider adding them as knowledge entries in Manus for quick access

4. Use consistently:

- Begin each session for this function with your specialized prompt
- Maintain consistency in how you frame requests for this function
- Reference the same knowledge entries each time

5. Refine over time:

- Note what works well and what could be improved
- Update your specialized prompt templates based on your experience
- Add new relevant information to your knowledge entries

By creating distinct specialized approaches for different marketing functions, you establish a more systematic approach to your AI-assisted marketing efforts.

Creating a System of Specialized AI Approaches

While you might start with a single, general-purpose approach to AI marketing assistance, consider developing these specialized approaches as your comfort level increases:

Content Creation Approach

- Focused on: Writing blog posts, social media content, email campaigns, and ad copy
- Specialized knowledge: Brand voice guidelines, successful content examples, audience language preferences
- Example prompt: *"You are my content creation assistant. Please follow our brand voice guidelines that emphasize a friendly, educational tone with no technical jargon. Use our standard blog post structure with a compelling question as the headline, personal story in the introduction, three main points with subheadings, and an action-oriented conclusion. I need a blog post about [topic]."*

Research Approach

- Focused on: Gathering market intelligence, competitor analysis, and trend identification
- Specialized knowledge: Research methodologies, competitor profiles, industry sources
- Example prompt: "You are my research assistant. When analyzing competitors, please evaluate their pricing strategy, unique selling proposition, content approach, and customer sentiment. Present findings in our standard competitive analysis format with strengths, weaknesses, opportunities, and threats

clearly identified. I need research on [competitor/ topic]."

Customer Service Approach

- Focused on: Drafting responses to customer inquiries, creating FAQs, developing service scripts
- Specialized knowledge: Common customer questions, policy details, tone guidelines for service communications
- Example prompt: "You are my customer service assistant. When drafting responses to customer inquiries, please maintain our empathetic but efficient tone, acknowledge the customer's concern specifically, provide a clear solution, and end with our standard closing that invites further questions if needed. Help me respond to this customer inquiry: [inquiry]."

Analytics Approach

- Focused on: Interpreting data, identifying patterns, generating insights from marketing metrics
- Specialized knowledge: Performance benchmarks, measurement frameworks, historical trends
- Example prompt: *"You are my analytics assistant. When reviewing campaign performance, please compare against our historical benchmarks, identify the top three factors influencing results, and provide specific, actionable recommendations for improvement based on the data. Analyze these campaign results: [data]."*

The key to success with specialized AI approaches is consistency—using the same prompt structure, instructions, and reference materials for each type of marketing task. This consistency allows you to develop increasingly effective specialized approaches over time.

How Specialized AI Approaches Work Together

You will be the coordinator between these specialized approaches. For example:

1. You might use your research approach to identify a market opportunity

2. You then manually take those insights to your content creation approach to create targeted content

3. After publishing, you use your analytics approach to evaluate performance

4. Based on those insights, you might return to your content creation approach with refinements

While this requires your active coordination, it creates a more systematic and effective marketing process than using a general-purpose approach for everything.

Getting Started: Simple First Steps

The concepts of knowledge bases and specialized AI approaches might seem advanced, but you can start small and expand over time:

1. **Begin with one knowledge category** that would most benefit your current marketing focus. For many small businesses, brand voice guidelines or customer personas are excellent starting points.

2. **Document as you go** rather than trying to build comprehensive knowledge bases all at once. Each time you create something valuable with your AI agent, save it to your knowledge base.

3. **Start with a general approach** and only develop specialized approaches for marketing functions you use frequently. Many small business owners begin with a content creation approach since content generation is often their most common AI use case.

4. **Be consistent in your approach** to each marketing function, using similar instructions and references each time. This consistency will naturally evolve into specialized approaches.

Practical Exercise: Your First Knowledge Base Entry

To put these concepts into practice, create your first knowledge base entry following these steps:

1. Log into your Manus account

2. Click on your name at the bottom left corner of the interface

3. Select "Knowledge" from the menu that appears

4. Click the "Add knowledge" button in the top right corner

5. Name your knowledge entry (e.g., "Brand Voice Guidelines")

6. In the "Manus will uses this knowledge when..." field, enter "discussing brand voice, creating content, or drafting marketing messages"

7. In the "Content" field, enter your current brand voice guidelines or preferences

8. Ensure the "Enabled" toggle is switched on

9. Click "Save" to create your knowledge entry

10. In a new conversation with Manus, ask a question related to your brand voice to test the effectiveness of your knowledge entry

This simple exercise begins the valuable practice of documenting and leveraging your business's specific information, which will enhance all the marketing techniques explored in subsequent chapters.

As we move forward in this book, remember that knowledge bases and specialized AI approaches are tools to enhance your marketing efforts—not requirements for success. You can implement these concepts gradually as your comfort level with AI marketing increases, focusing first on the approaches that offer the most immediate value for your specific business needs.

In the next chapter, we will explore how your AI agent can assist with market research, a foundational element of effective marketing strategy. The knowledge bases you begin building now will become increasingly valuable as you progress through more advanced marketing applications.

CHAPTER 3

Deep Dive into Market Research with an AI Agent

In the previous chapter, we explored the core capabilities of an AI marketing agent like Manus. Now, we're going to discuss one of the most critical foundations of any successful marketing strategy: **market research**. For small business owners, understanding your market landscape, competitors, and potential customers is not just beneficial – it's essential for survival and growth. You might be familiar with how general AI tools like GPT can assist with information gathering, but this chapter will focus on how a specialized Agent like Manus can become your dedicated market research powerhouse.

Market research can often feel like a daunting task, especially when resources are limited. However, with an Agent by your side, you can efficiently gather vast amounts of data, uncover hidden insights, and make informed decisions that drive your business forward. This chapter will guide you through the practical ways your Agent can help you understand your industry, analyze competitors, and ultimately, find your unique place in the market. We'll cover how to formulate effective research questions for your Agent and interpret the information it provides, turning raw data into actionable strategies.

Let's begin by exploring how your Agent can help you analyze your competitors, a crucial first step in understanding the environment in which your business operates. A key part of this analysis involves understanding their Strengths, Weaknesses, Opportunities, and Threats (SWOT). Your Agent can be particularly effective in researching the external factors – the "Opportunities" and "Threats" sections. For example, you can ask the Agent to research news articles, industry reports, or customer reviews related to a competitor to uncover potential weaknesses (e.g., poor customer service mentions, outdated technology) or external threats (e.g., new regulations impacting them, emerging disruptive technologies in their space).

Finding Gaps and Opportunities: Where Can Your Business Shine?

One of the most valuable outcomes of competitive analysis is the identification of market gaps or underserved needs that your small business can strategically address. By understanding what competitors are doing well, where they are lacking, and what customers are still looking for, you can carve out a unique position for your brand. Your Agent can assist in this process by synthesizing the information gathered about competitors and market trends, helping you to pinpoint these potential opportunities.

- **Prompt Example for Your Agent:** "*Based on the analysis of [Competitor A - e.g., their focus on high-end features and pricing] and [Competitor B - e.g., their limited product range], and considering current market trends in [your industry, e.g., a growing demand for budget-friendly, sustainable options], what are some potential underserved customer needs or market gaps that my small business, which aims to offer [your intended* *positioning, e.g., affordable and eco-conscious products], could address? List 3-5 potential opportunities with brief justifications."*

Understanding Your Target Industry Landscape with Your AI Agent

Beyond direct competitors, a comprehensive understanding of the broader industry landscape is vital. This includes factors like market size and growth potential, key segments within the market, regulatory environments, and potential partnership opportunities. Your Agent can be a valuable research assistant in exploring these areas:

- **Researching Market Size, Growth Potential, and Segmentation:** The agent can search for publicly available data and reports that provide estimates of market size, historical growth rates, and future projections for your industry or specific niches within it. It can also help identify how the market is typically segmented (e.g., by demographics, psychographics, geography, behavior).
- **Identifying Key Regulations, Compliance Issues, or Barriers to Entry:** Depending on your industry, there may be specific regulations, licensing requirements, or compliance standards that you need to be aware of. Your Agent can help research these, as well as common barriers to entry for new businesses in your sector (e.g., high capital requirements, strong brand loyalty to existing players, complex supply chains).
- **Exploring Potential Partnerships, Collaborations, or Distribution Channels:** The agent can help identify other businesses, organizations, or influencers

in your industry or complementary sectors that could be potential partners for collaboration, co-marketing, or distribution.

Example Prompts For Understanding Your Target Industry

Market Research:

AI Agent Prompt Example:

"I'm evaluating a new business opportunity in the boutique fitness industry, specifically targeting women over 40. Build a market research brief that includes: (1) estimated U.S. market size, (2) annual growth rate over the past 5 years, (3) projected growth for the next 3 years, and (4) common market segmentation breakdowns (demographics, psychographics, geography, behavior). Include links to any public sources or summaries from credible reports. After that, flag any promising niche segments and trends I should explore further."

Key Regulation/Compliance or Barriers to Entry

AI Agent Prompt Example:

"*Continue building the market research brief for the boutique fitness business targeting women over 40. Now focus on regulations, compliance issues, and barriers to entry in the U.S. fitness industry. Identify any state or federal licensing requirements for group fitness studios, health or liability regulations, insurance mandates, and ADA compliance. Also analyze common barriers to entry like startup capital, existing brand dominance, lease/rental issues, and hiring qualified trainers. Organize findings into a bulleted summary with links to source material. At the end, give me a quick-read risk assessment.*"

Exploring Potential Partnerships/ Collaborations/ Distribution Channels

AI Agent Prompt Example:

"Based on the target market of women over 40 and the boutique fitness industry, identify potential partnership opportunities. Look for complementary local businesses (e.g., wellness spas, nutritionists, activewear brands), national organizations focused on women's health, and relevant influencers with high engagement in the 40+ fitness space. Prioritize those with established audiences and aligned values. Also explore possible distribution or referral channels like community centers, online platforms, or corporate wellness programs. Present findings in three categories: Local Partners, National/Online Partners, and Distribution Channels. Include brief descriptions and links where possible."

Synthesizing Research into Actionable Insights: From Data to Decisions

Gathering information is only half the battle; the real value lies in synthesizing that information into actionable insights that can inform your business strategy. An Agent can be particularly helpful in this stage by summarizing large volumes of research data it has gathered, extracting key themes, and presenting findings in a more digestible format. For instance, after conducting extensive research on multiple competitors and market trends, you can ask the agent to create a concise summary report highlighting the most critical takeaways.

This synthesized information then becomes the foundation for your strategic decisions. It can help you refine your business plan, develop more targeted marketing messages, make informed product development choices, and ultimately, navigate the market with greater confidence and clarity.

Synthesizing Data Example Prompt

"I have gathered research data on [Insert your specific research topic here. For example: 'my top 3 online competitors and their marketing strategies,' or 'customer preferences for sustainable packaging in the specialty coffee industry,' or 'current trends in online fitness coaching for busy professionals.']."

I need your help to synthesize this information into a clear and actionable format. Please perform the following tasks based on the research data you have access to or that I have provided:

1. Summarize Key Findings: Provide a concise overview of the most important information and discoveries from the research.
2. Identify Main Themes & Patterns: What are the recurring themes, significant patterns, or notable trends that emerge from the collected data.
3. Highlight Critical Takeaways: Pinpoint the 2-3 most crucial pieces of information or conclusions that are directly relevant to my small business. For context, my business is [*Briefly describe your business and its primary goals here. For example: 'a newly launched online boutique selling handmade eco-friendly jewelry, aiming to increase brand awareness and initial sales,' or 'an established local bakery looking to expand its vegan product line and attract a younger demographic.'*].
4. Suggest Actionable Insights & Recommendations: Based on your synthesis, propose 3-5 actionable insights or strategic recommendations. For each one,

please explain how it could help my business make better decisions, such as refining marketing messages, improving product offerings, identifying new market opportunities, or addressing potential threats.

Please present this synthesized information (summary, themes, takeaways, and actionable insights) in a clear, organized, and easily digestible format, such as a bulleted list or a structured report."

Practical Exercise: Conduct a Mini Market Research Project for Your Business Using Your Agent

To put these concepts into practice, undertake a focused market research project for your own business or a business idea. Follow these steps:

1. **Define Your Objective:** Choose one specific research question you want to answer (e.g., "Who are my top 3 online competitors and what are their primary marketing strategies?").
2. **Formulate Prompts:** Develop a series of clear, specific prompts for your Agent to gather the necessary information related to your objective.
3. **Engage Your Agent:** Input your prompts and review the information provided by the agent.
4. **Refine and Iterate:** If the initial results are too broad or not specific enough, refine your prompts and ask follow-up questions to delve deeper.
5. **Synthesize Findings:** Ask your Agent to help summarize the key findings from its research.

6. **Draw Conclusions:** Based on the synthesized information, draw your own conclusions and identify at least one actionable insight for your business.

Pro-Tip: Iterative Research – Continuously Updating Your Market Knowledge with Your Agent

Market conditions, competitor activities, and consumer preferences are not static; they are constantly evolving. Therefore, market research should not be a one-time event but an ongoing process. Schedule regular check-ins with your Agent to research updates on key trends, monitor competitor activities, or explore new customer sentiments. This iterative approach will ensure that your business remains agile, responsive, and consistently aligned with the realities of your market, allowing you to adapt and thrive in the long term.

CHAPTER 4

Dialing in Your Perfect Customer Avatar with an AI Agent

If market research is the compass for your business, then understanding your ideal customer is the detailed map that guides your every marketing move. In a world saturated with messages, generic marketing that tries to appeal to everyone ultimately appeals to no one. The key to cutting through the noise and achieving real connection lies in deeply understanding precisely who you are trying to reach. This is where the concept of a customer avatar – a semi-fictional, detailed representation of your ideal customer – becomes an indispensable tool. This chapter will guide you through the process of researching and defining these crucial customer avatars, demonstrating how your Agent can significantly streamline and enhance this vital strategic exercise.

The Power of Knowing "Who": Why Customer Avatars are Essential for Targeted Marketing

Many small businesses make the mistake of casting too wide a net, believing that a larger audience equates to more potential sales. However, this approach often dilutes marketing efforts, wastes resources, and results in messaging that fails to resonate. A customer avatar, also known as a buyer persona, helps you move beyond vague demographic descriptions (e.g., "women aged 25-45") to a rich, nuanced understanding of a specific individual who represents your ideal client.

Why is this so powerful? Because a well-defined avatar informs virtually every aspect of your marketing strategy and even your product or service development. It helps you:

- **Craft Resonant Messaging:** When you know your avatar's specific pain points, aspirations, language, and motivations, you can tailor your marketing messages to speak directly to them in a way that feels personal and relevant.
- **Choose the Right Channels:** Understanding where your avatar spends their time online and offline allows you to focus your marketing budget and efforts on the channels where they are most likely to see and engage with your content.
- **Develop Relevant Content:** Your avatar's challenges and interests become a goldmine for content ideas (blog posts, videos, social media updates) that provide genuine value and position you as a helpful authority.
- **Guide Product/Service Development:** Insights into your avatar's unmet needs can directly influence how you design, refine, or package your offerings to better solve their problems.
- **Improve Sales Conversions:** When your marketing speaks directly to the right person with the right message at the right time, your sales efforts become far more effective.

In essence, customer avatars transform your marketing from a guessing game into a targeted, empathetic, and ultimately more successful endeavor.

Gathering the Raw Materials: Researching Your Ideal Customer with Your Agent

Creating an effective avatar isn't about guesswork; it's about research. Your Agent can be an invaluable assistant in gathering the diverse data points needed to build a comprehensive profile of your ideal customer.

Analyzing Your Existing Customer Base (If Applicable)

If you already have customers, they are your primary source of information. Look for common characteristics among your best customers – those who are most profitable, easiest to work with, and most enthusiastic about your offerings. If you have customer data in a digital format (e.g., a spreadsheet from your CRM or sales records, with personal identifying information anonymized or handled according to privacy regulations), your Agent can help you process this data to identify patterns in demographics, purchase history, or feedback. You would need to provide this data to the agent in a structured way it can understand.

Leveraging Online Research: Forums, Social Media, and Review Sites

The internet is a vast repository of conversations and opinions. Your Agent can efficiently scan online forums (like Reddit or Quora), relevant social media groups, and customer review sites (for your business or your competitors) to understand what people in your target market are discussing. This can reveal common questions, frustrations, desired outcomes, the language they use, and the solutions they are seeking.

- **Prompt Example for Your Agent:** "*Search online forums (e.g., specific subreddits related to [your product/service category, like r/homebrewing]) and social media groups (e.g., Facebook groups for [your target interest, like 'sustainable living enthusiasts']). What are the most common questions, challenges, and desired solutions people discuss related to [the problem your product/service solves, e.g., 'making high-quality craft beer at home' or 'reducing household plastic waste']? Summarize key themes.*"
- **Prompt Example for Your Agent:** "*Analyze customer reviews for [a popular competitor product/service, e.g., 'Brand X Organic Meal Kit Delivery']. What are the most frequently mentioned positive aspects and negative complaints? What unmet needs or desires are implied in these reviews?*"

Identifying Demographic Data

Demographics provide the basic factual outline of your avatar. This includes age, gender, location (general area, urban/rural), occupation, income level, education, and family status. Your Agent can help research general demographic trends associated with interest in your product or service category, or analyze demographic data you provide from your own customer base.

Uncovering Psychographic Data

Psychographics reveal the "why" behind your avatar's behavior. This is where you explore their values, beliefs, attitudes, interests, lifestyle, personality traits, and motivations. This deeper understanding is crucial for crafting truly resonant messaging. Your Agent can assist by researching articles, studies, or discussions that shed light on the psychographic profiles of consumers interested in your niche.

- **Prompt Example for Your Agent:** "*Research common values, interests, and lifestyle characteristics associated with individuals who are passionate about [e.g., 'adventure travel' or 'mindfulness and meditation']. Look for information on their motivations and priorities.*"

Building Your Avatar Profile: The Key Components

Once you have gathered your research, it's time to synthesize it into a detailed avatar profile. Here are the essential components:

1. **Name and a Face:** Give your avatar a memorable name (e.g., "Eco-Conscious Emily," "Tech-Savvy Tom"). Finding a stock photo that visually represents them can also make the avatar feel more real and relatable for you and your team.
2. **Detailed Demographics:** List out their age, gender, location, occupation, income, education, family situation, etc.
3. **Goals & Aspirations:** What are they trying to achieve in relation to your product/service, or in their broader life where your offering plays a role? What are their dreams and ambitions?
4. **Challenges & Pain Points:** What problems, frustrations, fears, or obstacles are they facing that your product or service can help them overcome? Be specific.

5. **Values, Beliefs, and Motivations:** What principles guide their decisions? What do they believe in? What internally or externally motivates them?
6. **Information Sources & Preferred Communication Channels:** Where do they get their information? Which blogs, social media platforms, publications, or influencers do they follow? How do they prefer to be communicated with (e.g., email, social media, phone)?
7. **Common Objections & Concerns:** What potential reasons might they have for not buying your product or service? What are their hesitations or skepticism?
8. **Crafting a "Day in the Life" Narrative:** Write a short story describing a typical day for your avatar. This helps to bring them to life and understand their context.
9. **Quotes or Catchphrases:** Include a few direct quotes (real ones from research if possible, or representative ones you create) that capture their mindset, challenges, or desires.

Using Your Agent to Draft and Refine Your Avatar Profiles

Your Agent can be a significant help in drafting the initial avatar profile based on the research data you've collected (or that it has helped you gather). You can provide the agent with your summarized research findings and ask it to structure them into an avatar template.

- **Prompt Example for Your Agent:** "*Based on the following research findings [summarize your key demographic, psychographic, goals, and pain point data here, or refer to a document you've compiled], draft a detailed customer avatar* *profile for a small business offering [your product/service, e.g., 'online courses for learning Spanish']. The avatar should be named 'Learner Laura.' Include sections for: Demographics, Goals & Aspirations, Challenges & Pain Points, Values & Motivations, Information Sources, and Common Objections. Also, write a brief 'Day in the Life' narrative for her."*

Don't expect the first draft to be perfect. The real power comes in the iteration. Review the AI-generated draft, identify areas that need more detail or nuance, and then ask your follow-up questions or provide more specific instructions to refine the profile. For example, if the "Pain Points" section is too generic, you might prompt: "*For Learner Laura's avatar, expand on her pain points related to learning a new language. What specific frustrations might she experience with traditional methods or time constraints?*"

Creating Multiple Avatars (If Necessary)

While you should start with your primary avatar, some businesses serve multiple distinct customer segments. If this is the case, you may need to create two or three different avatars. However, avoid creating too many, as this can dilute your focus. Each avatar should represent a significant and distinct group that requires a tailored marketing approach.

Validating Your Avatars: Ensuring They Reflect Real Customers

An avatar is only useful if it accurately reflects real people. Once you have drafted your avatar(s), take steps to validate them:

- **Talk to Real People:** If possible, interview some of your existing ideal customers or people who fit your avatar profile. Do their experiences, goals, and challenges align with what you've documented? Your Agent can help you draft interview questions.

- **Surveys:** Conduct surveys with your audience or a targeted group to gather quantitative data that can confirm or refine your avatar's characteristics. Again, your Agent can assist in drafting survey questions.
- **Compare with Actual Customer Interactions:** Review customer service logs, sales call notes, and social media interactions. Does the language and behavior of your real customers match your avatar?

Bringing Your Avatars to Life: How to Use Them in Daily Marketing Decisions

Your customer avatars shouldn't just be documents that gather dust. They should be active tools used in your daily marketing decisions. Before creating any new piece of content, launching a campaign, or even writing an email, ask yourself: "How would [Avatar's Name] react to this? Does this address their needs? Is this message in a place they would see it and in a language they would understand?" Share your avatars with your team (if you have one) to ensure everyone is aligned on who you are serving.

Practical Exercise: Create Your Primary Customer Avatar with Your Agent

1. **Choose Your Focus:** Decide on the primary ideal customer you want to create an avatar for.
2. **Gather Data:** Use your Agent (with the example prompts provided) to research demographics, psychographics, goals, and pain points relevant to this customer type and your business offering.

3. **Compile Findings:** Organize the research data into key themes.
4. **Draft with Your Agent:** Use a prompt similar to the example above to have your Agent draft the initial avatar profile.
5. **Refine and Elaborate:** Review the draft. Add details, make it more specific, and use your own insights. If needed, ask your Agent follow-up questions to flesh out certain sections.
6. **Give it a Name and Face:** Finalize the avatar with a name and a representative image.
7. **Consider Validation Steps:** Think about how you could validate this avatar with real customer interactions or further research.

Pro-Tip: Keep Your Avatars Updated – They Evolve as Your Market Does

Your customers and your market are not static. Periodically revisit and update your customer avatars (perhaps annually, or when you notice significant market shifts) to ensure they remain accurate and relevant. Your Agent can assist in this ongoing research process, helping you keep your finger on the pulse of your ideal customer.

CHAPTER 5

Defining Your Brand Voice: The Foundation for Your AI Marketing Assistant

Now that you have identified your target audience, the next essential step is to define *how* it will communicate with that audience. This is the essence of brand voice. In an era where artificial intelligence plays an increasingly significant role in content generation, a clearly articulated brand voice is not merely a stylistic preference but a strategic imperative. It is the core directive that ensures all AI-assisted communications—from website copy and email campaigns to social media updates—are authentic, consistent, and truly reflective of the business's unique identity and values. Without this foundational clarity, even the most sophisticated AI can produce content that feels generic or, worse, misaligned with the brand it intends to represent. This chapter provides a direct, value-driven approach for you to define your distinct brand voice and effectively instruct Manus to adopt it, transforming the AI agent into a genuine extension of your brand.

Understanding the Core of Your Brand Voice

Before instructing Manus, it is vital to dissect what constitutes a compelling brand voice. This understanding allows for a more deliberate and effective definition process. The primary components include the tone of communication, the specific language and vocabulary chosen, and the overarching personality or character the brand projects.

Tone of Communication

The tone refers to the overall attitude or emotional character conveyed through the brand's language. It significantly shapes audience perception. A brand might opt for a tone that is professional and authoritative, thereby building confidence; empathetic and supportive, fostering connection; or perhaps innovative and forward-thinking, inspiring excitement. While the fundamental tone should remain consistent to build recognition, slight modulations can be appropriate for different contexts—for example, a more formal tone for a detailed proposal versus a more engaging one for a community update. The selection of primary tones should be a strategic decision, aligning with the brand's objectives and the audience's expectations.

Language and Word Choice

This element encompasses the specific words, phrasing, sentence structures, and the general complexity of the language used. It also involves decisions about employing industry-specific terminology. For businesses addressing a specialized audience, technical language might be necessary and expected. However, for those targeting a broader demographic, clarity, conciseness, and easily understandable language are paramount. The guiding principle must always be effective communication, ensuring the chosen language conveys the intended message without ambiguity. Vocabulary choices should also reflect the desired level of formality and the nature of the relationship the brand seeks to build with its customers.

Reflecting Your Brand's Character

Brand personality involves attributing a set of human-like characteristics to the brand, making it more relatable, memorable, and distinct. Does the business wish to be perceived as an expert guide, a creative pioneer, a steadfast partner, or an insightful advisor? Defining these core personality traits provides a consistent character for Manus to embody. This ensures that all AI-generated interactions feel coherent and align with the persona the business aims to project, strengthening brand identity.

A Practical Approach to Articulating Your Voice

Defining a brand voice is a multi-step process. It begins with introspection about your business's core identity and your relationship with your audience, and culminates in a clear set of guidelines for all communications, including those generated by Manus.

Aligning Voice with Audience and Values

An authentic brand voice must be deeply rooted in the business's core values and finely tuned to the target audience identified in Chapter 3. Revisit the ideal customer profile: What are their communication preferences? What language resonates with them? What kind of interaction do they expect? Simultaneously, consider the fundamental principles that drive the business. The brand voice must be a genuine expression of these values, speaking directly to the intended audience in a manner they understand and appreciate.

Identifying Core Voice Descriptors

Translate the understanding of audience and values into specific attributes. This involves defining both desired characteristics and those to avoid:

- **Positive Voice Descriptors:** Identify three to five core adjectives or descriptive phrases that accurately characterize the desired brand voice. These should capture the essence of how the brand aims to be perceived (e.g., "Authoritative yet accessible," "Clear and pragmatic," "Innovative and insightful").
- **Voice Exclusions:** Conversely, list three to five characteristics the brand voice should *not* embody (e.g., "Overly academic," "Aggressively sales-oriented," "Vague or non-committal").

Guiding Word Choice for Consistency

Establish clear guidelines for vocabulary to ensure consistency and reinforce the desired tone:

- **Preferred Terminology:** List specific words, phrases, or types of language congruent with the brand (e.g., industry-specific terms if appropriate, positive language, phrases reflecting unique selling points).
- **Terminology to Avoid:** List words, jargon, or clichés to be excluded (e.g., overly technical terms unless defined, hype, outdated phrases).

Practical Exercise: Creating Your Brand Voice Reference Guide

To consolidate these elements into an actionable tool, create a concise Brand Voice Reference Guide. This document (typically 1-2 pages) serves as an internal standard and a crucial briefing tool for Manus. It should clearly outline:

1. **Brand Personality Summary:** (3-4 key adjectives defining the brand's character, e.g., Knowledgeable, Reliable, Client-Focused).
2. **Primary Tone(s) of Voice:** (e.g., Informative and professional, with a supportive undercurrent).
3. **Language Style Notes:** (e.g., Clear, direct, explains technical terms simply, maintains a professional cadence, avoids colloquialisms).
4. **Key Vocabulary Examples:** (List 5-7 preferred terms/phrases; List 5-7 terms/phrases to avoid).
5. **Illustrative Paragraph (Recommended):** A short paragraph (50-100 words) written in the desired brand voice, perhaps a mission statement excerpt or a value proposition, to provide a concrete example.

This Reference Guide is a vital asset for ensuring clarity and consistency in all brand communications, especially when directing any type of GPT or Agent.

Communicating Your Brand Voice to Manus

With a Brand Voice Reference Guide established, the next step is to effectively transfer these guidelines to Manus. This ensures that your agent can internalize and consistently apply the defined voice.

Providing Manus with Initial Voice Instructions

When initiating a new project or a series of content tasks with Manus, a comprehensive initial briefing on brand voice is essential. This prompt should clearly articulate the core personality, tone, language style, and vocabulary requirements, referencing the Brand Voice Reference Guide.

- **Prompt Example for Manus:** "*Manus, for all content related to our [e.g., new client onboarding materials for our financial advisory service], strict adherence to our Brand Voice Reference Guide is required. Key parameters include:*

****Brand Personality:** *e.g., Trustworthy, Expert, and Proactive.*

****Primary Tone:** *e.g., Professional, Clear, and Reassuring.*

****Language Style:** *e.g., Direct, avoiding jargon where possible, or explaining financial terms concisely for a non-expert audience. Maintain a respectful and supportive cadence.*

****Preferred Vocabulary:** *e.g., long-term financial planning, wealth management strategies, secure future.*

****Avoid:** *e.g., get rich quick, guaranteed returns, overly casual or familiar language. Please begin by drafting a welcome letter to a new client, outlining the initial steps in our advisory process, ensuring it fully embodies these voice characteristics.*"

Leveraging Your Brand Voice Reference with Manus

The Brand Voice Reference Guide is a dynamic tool. For ongoing projects, periodically remind Manus of these guidelines or paste relevant sections into prompts for specific tasks, especially if nuanced application is needed for different content types (e.g., a detailed market analysis versus a brief service update).

Refining Manus's Understanding Through Feedback

Teaching Manus your brand voice is an iterative process. Review initial outputs against the Reference Guide and provide specific, constructive feedback.

- **Example of Constructive Feedback:** "Manus, the draft welcome letter is informative. However, the tone in the third paragraph is slightly more passive than our **proactive** personality trait suggests. Please revise to convey more initiative and confidence in guiding the client, as per our voice guidelines. Also, ensure all technical terms are briefly defined as per our language style notes."

This detailed feedback enables Manus to learn and progressively improve its application of your brand's unique voice.

Ensuring Long-Term Voice Integrity

Maintaining brand voice consistency with AI assistance requires ongoing diligence.

The Indispensable Role of Human Oversight

While Manus can adeptly learn and apply voice guidelines, human judgment remains paramount. You are the ultimate steward of your brand. All AI-generated content should undergo a final human review to ensure voice adherence, strategic alignment, and contextual appropriateness. This guarantees your brand's message is always accurate and truly representative.

Adapting Your Voice Over Time

Brands evolve. Periodically review and update your Brand Voice Reference Guide to reflect any shifts in market positioning, audience, or business strategy. Communicate these updates clearly to Manus to ensure it operates from the most current voice parameters.

CHAPTER 6

Unleashing Creativity: Idea Generation and Unique Research Methods with an AI Agent

In the competitive arena of small business marketing, fresh ideas and innovative approaches are not just desirable – they are often the differentiators that capture attention and drive growth. However, maintaining a consistent flow of creativity can be challenging, especially when juggling the myriad responsibilities of running a business. This chapter explores how your Agent can transcend its role as a data processor and information retriever to become a powerful creative catalyst and a partner in unconventional research, helping you break through marketing ruts, generate novel ideas, and discover unique insights.

Your AI Agent as a Creative Catalyst: Breaking Through Marketing Ruts

Many small business owners find themselves stuck in familiar patterns, relying on the same marketing tactics year after year. While consistency has its merits, a lack of fresh thinking can lead to stagnation and missed opportunities. An Agent can help inject new energy into your creative processes, not by replacing human ingenuity, but by augmenting and stimulating it. It can offer diverse perspectives, rapidly generate a multitude of starting points, and help you explore avenues you might not have considered on your own.

The key is to approach your Agent as a brainstorming partner. It doesn't get tired, it doesn't have preconceived notions (beyond its training data), and it can access and combine information in ways that can spark unexpected connections. By leveraging its capabilities, you can overcome creative blocks and foster a more dynamic and innovative marketing mindset.

Brainstorming Marketing Campaign Ideas with Your AI Agent

Coming up with compelling marketing campaign themes that resonate with your target audience and align with your business goals is a critical creative task. Your Agent can be an excellent resource for generating a wide range of initial ideas, which you can then refine and develop.

- **Generating Diverse Campaign Themes and Concepts:** Whether you're planning a seasonal promotion, a brand-building initiative, or a product launch, your Agent can help brainstorm various themes. You can provide it with context about your business, your target avatar (as developed in Chapter 3), your objectives, and any specific constraints (like budget or timeline).
    - **Prompt Example for Your Agent:** *"I run a small, independent bookstore specializing in local authors and community events. My target avatar is "Literary Lisa," a woman aged 35-55 who values community connection and unique literary experiences. Brainstorm 10*

unique marketing campaign ideas for the upcoming summer season, with a budget under $1000, focusing on increasing foot traffic and local engagement. For each idea, suggest a core theme and a key activity."

- **Developing Catchy Taglines, Slogans, and Campaign Names:** Once you have a campaign theme, crafting memorable language is crucial. Your Agent can generate multiple options for taglines, slogans, or names that encapsulate the essence of your campaign and appeal to your avatar.
  - **Prompt Example for Your Agent**: "*For a marketing campaign themed around 'Discovering Local Literary Gems' for my independent bookstore, generate 15 catchy taglines and 5 potential campaign names that would appeal to Literary Lisa.*"

Content Topic Ideation: Never Run Out of Things to Say

Consistent, valuable content is essential for attracting and engaging your audience, whether it's through blog posts, social media updates, videos, or podcasts. However, constantly generating fresh topic ideas can be a significant hurdle. Your Agent can act as an inexhaustible idea generator for your content calendar.

- **Generating Blog Post Titles, Video Ideas, Podcast Topics, Social Media Themes:** Provide your Agent with your core business offerings, your target avatar's interests and pain points, and the types of content you want to create. It can then suggest a multitude of relevant and engaging topics.
  - **Prompt Example for Your Agent**: "*My business sells organic, handcrafted soaps. My target avatar, Eco-*

Conscious Emily, is interested in natural skincare, sustainability, and DIY beauty. Generate 20 blog post ideas, 10 short video ideas (for Instagram Reels/ TikTok), and 5 social media content themes that would appeal to her and provide practical value or inspiration."

- **Exploring Different Angles on a Core Topic:** Even with a core topic, your Agent can help you explore various angles, sub-topics, or formats to keep your content fresh and comprehensive.
  - **Prompt Example for Your Agent:** "*For the core topic of 'The Benefits of Natural Soap,' generate 5 different angles for blog posts, such as a scientific explanation, a personal story, a comparison with commercial soaps, a guide to choosing the right natural soap, and a DIY recipe angle.*"

Developing Your Unique Selling Proposition (USP) with Your AI Agent

Your Unique Selling Proposition (USP) is what makes your business stand out from the competition. It's the compelling reason why customers should choose you over others. Crafting a strong USP requires understanding your strengths, your competitors' weaknesses, and your target customer's deepest needs. Your Agent can assist in this strategic creative process.

- **Analyzing Competitor USPs and Identifying Your Differentiators:** As discussed in market research, your Agent can help you analyze what your competitors claim as their USPs. By comparing this with your own business's strengths (which you define) and the needs of your avatar, you can start to identify potential areas where you can uniquely shine.

- **Crafting a Compelling USP Statement:** Once you have a clearer idea of your unique angle, your Agent can help you brainstorm and refine a concise and impactful USP statement that clearly communicates your distinct value to your target audience.
  - **Prompt Example for Your Agent**: *"Help me brainstorm potential USPs for my online business that offers personalized, hand-painted pet portraits. My key differentiators are: [e.g., hyper-realistic style, use of eco-friendly paints, a portion of profits donated to animal shelters]. My target avatar is "Devoted Pet Parent David," who sees his pet as a family member and values high-quality, sentimental items. Generate 5-7 draft USP statements."*

Innovative Research Methods: Beyond Standard Searches

Beyond straightforward information retrieval, your Agent can facilitate more innovative and creative research approaches, helping you uncover insights that might be missed by traditional methods.

- **Sentiment Analysis (Conceptual):** While your Agent may not have a dedicated sentiment analysis tool, if you provide it with a collection of customer reviews (e.g., copied into the prompt) or social media comments, you can ask it to identify and summarize the general sentiment (positive, negative, neutral) and key themes expressed within that text. This can offer a quick pulse check on customer perceptions.

- **Prompt Example (Conceptual – requires you to provide the text):** "*I've pasted 20 customer reviews for my product below. Please read through them and summarize: 1. The overall sentiment (mostly positive, mixed, mostly negative). 2. The top 3 most frequently mentioned positive aspects. 3. The top 3 most frequently mentioned negative aspects or complaints.*"

- **Exploring Analogous Industries or Markets for Inspiration:** Sometimes, the best ideas come from looking outside your immediate industry. You can ask your Agent to research innovative marketing strategies, customer service approaches, or business models in completely different sectors that have faced similar challenges or served similar customer archetypes. This can spark fresh thinking for your own business.
  - **Prompt Example for Your Agent:** "*My small subscription box business for [e.g., gourmet snacks] is struggling with customer retention. Research innovative customer retention strategies used by successful subscription businesses in analogous industries like [e.g., software-as-a-service (SaaS) or beauty boxes]. What are 3-4 interesting tactics they use that could potentially be adapted?*"

- **"What If" Scenarios: Exploring Hypothetical Situations:** Use your Agent to play out hypothetical scenarios or explore creative solutions by posing "what if" questions. This can be a powerful way to challenge assumptions and brainstorm unconventional approaches.
  - **Prompt Example for Your Agent:** "*Imagine a local coffee shop that decided to completely eliminate disposable cups and operate on a 100% reusable cup*

model (either customers bring their own or use a deposit-return system). What are some unconventional marketing approaches they might take to promote this unique, sustainable model and educate their community? Brainstorm 5 creative ideas."

Overcoming Creative Blocks with Your AI Agent as Your Sounding Board

Every creative person experiences blocks. When you're stuck for an idea or unsure how to develop a concept, your Agent can act as a non-judgmental sounding board.

- **Refining Half-Baked Ideas:** If you have a nascent idea that isn't fully formed, describe it to your Agent and ask for suggestions on how to develop it, what potential challenges to consider, or what alternative directions it could take.
- **Asking for Alternative Perspectives or Critiques:** You can present an idea to your Agent and ask it to play devil's advocate or offer alternative viewpoints. For example: *"I'm considering a marketing campaign focused on [theme]. What are some potential downsides or criticisms of this approach I should consider? What alternative themes might achieve a similar goal for my target avatar?"*

Practical Exercise: Brainstorm a New Marketing Initiative for Your Business with Your Agent

1. **Identify a Need/Goal:** What's one marketing challenge you're facing or a new goal you want to achieve (e.g., increase social media engagement, launch a new product, attract a new customer segment)?

2. **Provide Context to Your Agent:** Clearly explain the challenge/goal, your business, your target avatar, and any constraints (budget, timeline, etc.).
3. **Brainstorm Initial Ideas:** Use a prompt to ask your Agent to generate a diverse set of initial ideas (e.g., campaign themes, content series, promotional offers).
4. **Select and Deepen:** Choose one or two of the most promising ideas generated by the agent.
5. **Refine with Your Agent:** Use follow-up prompts to ask the agent to help you flesh out the selected idea(s). Ask for specific suggestions for taglines, key messages, content formats, or potential activities.
6. **Consider Unconventional Angles:** Ask your Agent to suggest a unique or unexpected twist on the idea.
7. **Outline a Basic Concept:** Develop the idea into a brief concept outline that you could then develop further.

Pro-Tip: Combine AI Suggestions with Your Own Intuition and Industry Knowledge

Remember, your Agent is a tool to augment your creativity, not replace it. The most potent creative outcomes arise when you combine the diverse suggestions and rapid ideation capabilities of the AI with your own human intuition, industry experience, ethical judgment, and deep understanding of your brand's unique voice and values. Use the AI to broaden your horizons and generate possibilities, then apply your expertise to select, refine, and implement the ideas that truly resonate and align with your strategic objectives.

CHAPTER 7

Crafting Your Small Business Website with an AI Agent

In the digital age, your website is far more than just an online brochure; it is the central hub of your marketing efforts, your 24/7 digital storefront, and often the first impression potential customers have of your brand. For a small business, a professional, effective, and well-maintained website is not a luxury but a fundamental necessity for credibility, visibility, and growth. However, the prospect of creating or overhauling a website can seem overwhelming, particularly with limited technical expertise or budget. This chapter will discuss the process and demonstrate how your Agent can be an invaluable assistant in planning, creating content for, and even understanding some technical aspects of your small business website, empowering you to build a powerful online presence.

Note: Manus can build clean, content-rich websites that are ready to launch without the need for coding, hosting, or plugins—perfect for getting online fast. However, design and functionality are very limited, and the sites remain within the Manus ecosystem, which may not suit those needing full customization or external integrations.

Manus can also work with a web developer in terms of planning, content generation, research, and basic code understanding, making the overall process more manageable and efficient for you. And Manus built sites are a good way to test concepts quickly.

Your Website: The Digital Storefront and Hub of Your Marketing

Before we begin, let's reinforce why your website is so critical. An effective small business website serves multiple crucial functions:

- **Establishes Credibility and Professionalism:** A well-designed, informative website signals to potential customers that you are a legitimate and trustworthy business.
- **Provides Essential Information:** It's where customers can find out who you are, what you offer, how to contact you, and why they should choose you.
- **Generates Leads and Sales:** Your website can be a powerful tool for capturing leads, facilitating online sales (for e-commerce businesses), or driving customers to your physical location.
- **Builds Brand Awareness:** It's a platform to showcase your brand identity, tell your story, and differentiate yourself from competitors.
- **Serves as a Content Hub:** Your website can host your blog, case studies, testimonials, and other valuable content that attracts organic traffic and positions you as an expert.

Key elements of an effective small business website include clear and intuitive navigation, compelling and persuasive copy, strong calls to action (CTAs), mobile-friendliness (responsive design), fast loading speed, and basic search engine optimization (SEO) principles.

Planning Your Website Structure and User Experience (UX) with Your AI Agent

A successful website starts with a solid plan. Before you write a single line of code or choose a template, you need to define your website's goals and how it will serve your target audience. Your Agent can assist in this strategic planning phase.

- **Defining Website Goals:** What do you want your website to achieve for your business? Is it primarily to generate leads, sell products directly, provide information and resources, build brand awareness, or facilitate appointment bookings? Clearly articulating these goals will shape every subsequent decision.
- **Identifying Target Audience Actions:** Based on your customer avatars (Chapter 4) and your website goals, what specific actions do you want visitors to take on your site? (e.g., fill out a contact form, purchase a product, subscribe to a newsletter, read a blog post, watch a demo video).
- **Brainstorming Site Navigation and Key Pages:** Your Agent can help you brainstorm the essential pages your website will need and how they should be organized for intuitive navigation. Common key pages include: Homepage, About Us, Services/ Products (with individual pages for each if necessary), Blog, Contact Us, Privacy Policy, and Terms of Service.

– **Prompt Example for Your Agent:** "*Help me outline the key pages and a logical navigation structure for a website for my [type of business, e.g., 'local artisanal bakery specializing in custom cakes']. My main website goals are to showcase my cake designs, provide information about ordering, and encourage inquiries for custom orders. My target audience is primarily local individuals planning special events (birthdays, weddings, etc.).*"

- **Outlining User Flows and Basic Sitemaps:** For more complex sites, understanding how users will move through your website (user flows) is important. Your Agent can help you think through these paths and even assist in outlining a basic sitemap (a hierarchical list of your website's pages) to ensure clarity and logical organization before development begins.

Content is Queen (on Your Website Too!): Generating Website Copy with Your AI Agent

Compelling, persuasive, and informative content is the lifeblood of an effective website. This is an area where your Agent can provide immense value, helping you draft copy for various key pages. Remember to always review, edit, and infuse AI-generated copy with your unique brand voice and specific details.

- **Crafting Compelling Homepage Copy:** Your homepage is often the first page visitors see. It needs to grab their attention immediately, clearly communicate your value proposition (what you do and why it matters to them), and guide them towards the next step. Your Agent can help draft headlines, introductory paragraphs, and calls to action for your homepage.

- **Prompt Example for Your Agent:** "*Write compelling homepage copy for a small business called 'GreenThumb Landscaping.' The key message should be about creating beautiful, sustainable, and low-maintenance garden spaces for busy homeowners. The target audience values eco-friendly practices and expert design. Include a strong headline, a brief introductory paragraph (2-3 sentences), and a primary call to action.*"

- **Writing Engaging "About Us" Pages:** Your "About Us" page is an opportunity to build trust and connect with your audience on a more personal level by sharing your brand's story, mission, values, and the people behind it. Your Agent can help you structure this narrative and draft initial content.
- **Developing Persuasive Product/ Service Descriptions:** For your product or service pages, you need copy that not only describes what you offer but also highlights the benefits for the customer and persuades them to take action. Your Agent can help generate feature lists, benefit statements, and persuasive descriptions tailored to your target avatar's needs and pain points.

- **Prompt Example for Your Agent:** "*Generate an outline and draft copy for a services page for a 'Virtual Assistant for Solopreneurs' business. The services offered are: Email Management, Calendar Scheduling, Social Media Content Creation, and Basic Bookkeeping. For each service, suggest 2-3 key benefits to highlight for busy* *solopreneurs who are feeling overwhelmed and need to free up their time."*

- **Creating Informative FAQ Sections:** A well-structured Frequently Asked Questions (FAQ) page can save you time by proactively addressing common customer queries and can also improve user experience. Your Agent can help you brainstorm potential questions based on your offerings and then draft clear, concise answers.
- **Generating Blog Post Ideas, Outlines, and First Drafts:** As discussed in Chapter 5, your website's blog is crucial for attracting organic traffic and establishing authority. Your Agent can continue to be your partner in generating blog topic ideas, creating detailed outlines, and even writing initial drafts that you can then edit and personalize.

Visuals and Design: How Your AI Agent Can Assist (Conceptually)

While your Agent doesn't typically create visual designs or graphics itself (yet!), it can still assist in the conceptual phase of your website's visual identity.

- **Brainstorming Design Concepts, Color Palettes, and Branding Elements:** You can describe your brand personality, target audience, and industry to your Agent and ask it to suggest potential design aesthetics (e.g., minimalist, modern, rustic, playful), color palettes that evoke certain emotions, or types of imagery that might resonate.
- **Finding Inspiration for Website Layouts and Visual Styles:** Ask your Agent to research examples

of well-designed websites in your industry or in analogous fields that cater to a similar target audience. This can provide inspiration for layouts, visual hierarchies, and overall style. (You would then need to visit these sites yourself or with a designer).

Technical Aspects: Where Your AI Agent Can Assist

For many small business owners, the technical side of websites can be the most intimidating. While your Agent isn't a substitute for a skilled developer for complex needs, it can help you understand certain concepts and even assist with very basic tasks.

- **Understanding Different Website Platforms:** There are numerous platforms available for building websites (e.g., WordPress, Squarespace, Shopify for e-commerce, Wix). Choosing the right one depends on your needs, budget, and technical comfort level. Your Agent can research and summarize the pros, cons, features, and typical pricing for various platforms based on criteria you provide.
  - **Prompt Example for Your Agent:** "*Compare WordPress.com (hosted) and Squarespace for a small service-based business (e.g., a consultant) who needs a professional-looking portfolio website with a blog and contact form. Key considerations are ease of use for a non-technical person, design flexibility, and affordability. What are the main advantages and disadvantages of each in this context?*"
- **Basic HTML/CSS/JavaScript Understanding:** If you're using a platform that allows for some code customization, or if you encounter simple code

snippets you need to understand, your Agent can often act as a basic coding assistant. It might be able to explain what a piece of HTML code does, suggest simple CSS for styling adjustments, or help you understand a basic JavaScript function. It can also generate very simple code structures.

  - **Prompt Example for Your Agent:** "*Explain what this HTML code for creating a simple button does: [paste a short, simple HTML code snippet here].*"
  - **Prompt Example for Your Agent:** "*Provide a basic HTML and CSS structure for a webpage section that has a heading, a paragraph of text, and an image aligned to the right of the text.*"

- **SEO for Your Website: Laying the Groundwork:** Search Engine Optimization (SEO) is crucial for helping your website get found in search engine results. While a later chapter will go deeper into SEO, your Agent can help you with foundational aspects during website creation, such as identifying relevant keywords to incorporate into your website copy (based on your business and target audience) and ensuring your content is structured in an SEO-friendly way (e.g., proper use of headings).

Practical Exercise: Plan a Key Page for Your Website with Your Agent

1. **Choose a Key Page:** Select one important page for your website that you need to create or improve (e.g., Homepage, a specific Service page, About Us page).

2. **Define Objectives for the Page:** What is the primary goal of this page? What do you want visitors to do after viewing it?
3. **Gather Information with Your Agent:** Use prompts to ask your Agent for help in brainstorming content sections, key messages, and calls to action for this page, keeping your target avatar in mind.
4. **Draft the Copy with Your Agent:** Ask the agent to generate a first draft of the copy for the different sections of the page.
5. **Review and Refine:** Critically review the AI-generated copy. Edit it for clarity, accuracy, brand voice, and persuasiveness. Add your own unique insights and details.
6. **Consider Visuals (Conceptually):** Think about what kind of images or visual elements would complement the copy on this page. You can even ask your Agent for ideas on visual themes.

Pro-Tip: Your Website is a Living Entity – Plan for Ongoing Maintenance and Updates

Creating your website is just the beginning. An effective website requires ongoing maintenance, content updates, and periodic reviews to ensure it remains relevant, secure, and aligned with your business goals. Your Agent can continue to assist with generating fresh blog content, updating service descriptions, and researching new trends to keep your site current.

Note: If your website serves the public, ADA compliance matters—not just legally, but to ensure accessibility for all visitors. While Manus handles basic readability well, full ADA compliance (like screen reader optimization or keyboard navigation) may still require additional review or tools.

CHAPTER 8

Powering Your Email Marketing with an AI Agent

In an era dominated by fleeting social media trends and ever-changing search engine algorithms, email marketing remains a steadfast and remarkably effective pillar of small business communication and sales. Unlike rented audiences on social platforms, your email list is an asset you own, offering a direct line of communication to individuals who have explicitly expressed interest in your brand. When executed thoughtfully, email marketing boasts one of the highest returns on investment (ROI) of any marketing channel. This chapter will explore how your Agent can become a powerful ally in supercharging your email marketing efforts, from building your list and crafting compelling content to brainstorming campaign ideas and conceptualizing automation, all while maintaining a focus on delivering genuine value to your subscribers.

Email Marketing: Still a Powerhouse for Small Business Communication and Sales

Despite the rise of newer channels, email's enduring power lies in its directness, personalization potential, and the ability to nurture relationships over time. For small businesses, it offers several key advantages:

- **Direct Communication:** Email lands directly in your subscriber's inbox, a personal space where you can have a more focused conversation than on crowded public platforms.
- **Ownership of Your List:** Your email list is a valuable business asset, independent of third-party platform policies or algorithm changes. You control how and when you communicate with your audience.
- **High ROI:** Generally, email marketing is cost-effective, especially when compared to paid advertising, and can yield significant returns when done well.
- **Personalization Potential:** Email allows for deep segmentation and personalization, enabling you to send highly relevant messages that resonate with specific customer groups, leading to better engagement and conversions.
- **Nurturing Leads and Building Loyalty:** Email is ideal for guiding potential customers through the sales funnel, educating them about your offerings, and building lasting relationships with existing customers.

Building Your Email List (Ethically and Effectively)

The foundation of successful email marketing is a quality email list built with consent. Never buy email lists; focus on attracting subscribers organically who genuinely want to hear from you. Your Agent can be a creative partner in brainstorming effective lead magnets – valuable incentives offered in exchange for an email address.

Common lead magnet strategies include:

* **Valuable Content:** eBooks, guides, checklists, templates, whitepapers, or exclusive access to webinars or video content.

* **Discounts and Offers:** First-time purchase discounts, free shipping, or exclusive access to sales.

* **Tools and Resources:** Calculators, planners, or resource libraries.

* **Contests and Giveaways:** Offering a chance to win a product or service.

- **Prompt Example for Your AI Agent:** "*Brainstorm 5 compelling lead magnet ideas for a small business that offers [e.g., 'handmade organic skincare products']. The target avatar is 'Eco-Conscious Emily,' who values natural ingredients, sustainability, and self-care. The lead magnet should encourage sign-ups for our weekly newsletter which shares skincare tips and product updates.*"

Once you have lead magnet ideas, ensure you have clear sign-up forms on your website (e.g., in the header/footer, on blog posts, as pop-ups – used judiciously) and promote your newsletter on social media and other relevant channels. Always ensure your sign-up process is compliant with data privacy regulations like GDPR or CCPA, clearly stating what subscribers can expect.

Crafting Irresistible Subject Lines with Your AI Agent

The subject line is arguably the most critical element of your email. It's the first thing subscribers see and heavily influences whether they open your email or ignore it. With inboxes more crowded than ever, a compelling subject line is paramount. Your Agent can be an excellent tool for brainstorming multiple subject line variations, helping you experiment with different approaches.

Key techniques for writing compelling subject lines include:

* **Clarity and Conciseness:** Get straight to the point. Subscribers should understand what the email is about at a glance.

* **Curiosity:** Pique interest without being misleading (avoid clickbait).

* **Urgency and Scarcity:** Suggest timeliness without using red-flag language like "limited time offer" or "act now." Instead, opt for softer phrasing like "Ends Friday" or "Just added."

* **Benefit-Driven:** Highlight the value or solution the email offers.

* **Personalization:** Some companies swear by using the subscriber's name or referencing their interests but some feel that this tactic has lost its luster and can backfire. It might depend on your niche, test each and see your results.

* **Emojis (Used Sparingly and Appropriately):** Can help your email stand out but ensure they align with your brand and audience.

- **Prompt Example for Your AI Agent:** "*Generate 10 compelling and concise email subject lines for a promotional email announcing a [e.g., 'new collection of hand-poured soy candles']. The target audience is primarily women aged 25-55 who appreciate home decor and relaxation. Aim for a mix of subject lines that evoke curiosity, highlight benefits, and create a sense of newness. Keep them under 60 characters.*"

Always consider A/B testing different subject lines with your email marketing platform to see what resonates best with your specific audience.

Writing Engaging Email Content with Your AI Agent

Once your subject line gets the open, the email content must deliver on the promise and engage the reader. Your Agent can assist in drafting various types of email content, which you should then always review, personalize, and infuse with your unique brand voice.

Welcome Emails and Sequences

A welcome email (or a short series of them) is your first opportunity to make a great impression on new subscribers, confirm their subscription, deliver any promised lead magnet, and set expectations for future communications. It's crucial for building rapport from day one. Make sure your welcome message reflects the brand voice you defined in Chapter 3—this is where consistency begins.

- **Prompt Example for Your AI Agent:** "*Write a 3-part welcome email sequence for new subscribers to my [e.g., 'weekly gardening tips'] newsletter.*
  - *Email 1: Welcome the subscriber, thank them for joining, deliver the [lead magnet, e.g., 'Top 10 Low-Maintenance Plants Guide'], and briefly state what they can expect from the newsletter.*
  - *Email 2 (sent 2 days later): Share one highly valuable [e.g., 'gardening tip for beginners'] and invite them to follow us on social media.*

- *Email 3 (sent 4 days later): Introduce a popular product or service, or share a customer success story, and perhaps offer a small introductory discount."*

Promotional Emails That Convert

Promotional emails aim to drive sales or specific actions. To be effective, they should focus on the value and benefits for the customer, rather than just listing features. They need a clear call to action (CTA) and should avoid being overly salesy or spammy, which can lead to unsubscribes.

- **Prompt Example for Your AI Agent:** *"Draft a promotional email for a new online course on [e.g., 'Mastering Sourdough Baking for Beginners']. The target avatar is 'Home Baker Ben,' who is enthusiastic but often struggles with getting a good rise. Highlight 3-4 key benefits of the course that address his pain points. Include a clear call to action to 'Enroll Now' and mention a limited-time early bird discount."*

Newsletters That Build Community

Newsletters are excellent for keeping your brand top-of-mind, sharing valuable content (like blog post summaries, industry news, tips), building a sense of community, and subtly promoting your offerings. Consistency is key with newsletters.

Abandoned Cart Recovery Emails (for E-commerce)

If you run an e-commerce business, abandoned cart emails are a must. These automated emails remind customers about items they left in their cart and can significantly recover potentially lost sales. Your Agent can help draft persuasive copy for these, perhaps offering a small incentive to complete the purchase.

Personalization in Email

Personalization goes beyond just using the subscriber's first name. It involves tailoring content based on their past purchases, browsing history, engagement levels, or stated preferences (if you collect this data). While your Agent doesn't manage your customer data directly, if you provide it with information about a specific customer segment and their avatar, it can help you draft more targeted and relevant email copy for that group.

Designing Your Emails: Your AI Agent for Content Structure and Ideas

While your Agent typically doesn't design visual email templates (this is usually handled by your email marketing platform's editor or a designer), it can help you structure the content within your emails for maximum impact and readability.

- **Outlining the Logical Flow:** Ask your Agent to help you outline the sections of an email to ensure a clear and logical progression of information, leading effectively to the call to action.
- **Brainstorming Effective Calls to Action (CTAs):** Your Agent can generate various CTA phrases that are clear, concise, and action-oriented (e.g., "Shop Now," "Learn More," "Download Your Free Guide," "Claim Your Discount," "Register Today").

Segmenting Your Audience for Targeted Campaigns (Conceptual)

Sending the same email to everyone on your list is rarely the most effective approach. Segmentation involves dividing your list into smaller groups based on shared characteristics (e.g., demographics, purchase history, engagement level, interests) so you can send them more relevant and targeted messages. Your Agent can help you think through potential segmentation criteria if you describe the types of customer data you have available (e.g., from your CRM or e-commerce platform).

- **Prompt Example for Your AI Agent:** "*I have customer data that includes [e.g., 'purchase history (product categories bought)', 'date of last purchase', 'location (city/state)', and 'whether they opened the last 3 emails']. What are some potential ways I could segment my email list for my [e.g., 'online pet supply store'] to send more targeted promotional campaigns or content? Suggest 3-4 segmentation strategies with a brief rationale for each.*"

Automating Your Email Marketing: Your AI Agent for Workflow Ideas

Email automation allows you to send a series of pre-written emails triggered by specific subscriber actions or timelines. This saves time and ensures consistent communication. Your Agent can help you brainstorm ideas for various automation sequences (also known as drip campaigns).

Examples include:

* Welcome series (as discussed)

* Lead nurturing sequences (for subscribers who downloaded a lead magnet but haven't purchased)

* Post-purchase follow-ups (thanking customers, asking for reviews, offering complementary products)

* Re-engagement campaigns (for inactive subscribers)

* Birthday or anniversary emails

(Note: Your Agent helps with the content strategy and copy for these automations. The actual technical setup and integration will be done within your chosen email marketing platform.

Measuring Email Marketing Success: Key Metrics to Track

To understand what's working and where you can improve, you need to track key email marketing metrics. Most email marketing platforms provide detailed analytics. Important metrics include:

- **Open Rate:** Percentage of recipients who opened your email. While once a key benchmark, this is now considered a vanity metric—often inflated by bots or email previews that don't reflect real engagement. Use it cautiously and in context.
- **Click-Through Rate (CTR):** Percentage of recipients who clicked on one or more links in your email.
- **Conversion Rate:** Percentage of recipients who completed a desired action (e.g., made a purchase, filled out a form) after clicking a link.
- **Unsubscribe Rate:** Percentage of recipients who opted out of your email list.

- **Bounce Rate:** Percentage of emails that couldn't be delivered. High bounce rates—especially from hard bounces due to invalid addresses—can damage your sender reputation, trigger spam filters, and even land your domain on blacklists. Spam traps and outdated lists are common culprits, so regular list hygiene is essential.

If you can export this data in a processable format (e.g., a CSV file), your Agent might be able to help you analyze campaign results and summarize key findings or trends, although dedicated analytics tools are often more robust for this. Tools like NotebookLM, Looker Studio, or Supermetrics can help you visualize performance, spot patterns, and make data-driven decisions more efficiently.

Practical Exercise: Draft a Promotional Email with Your AI Agent

1. **Choose a Product/Service:** Select one of your offerings you want to promote.
2. **Define Your Goal & Avatar:** What's the goal of the email (e.g., drive sales, announce a new feature)? Who is your target avatar for this promotion?
3. **Brainstorm Subject Lines:** Use your Agent to generate 5-10 subject line options.
4. **Outline Email Content:** Ask your Agent to help you outline the key sections of the email (e.g., hook, problem/solution, benefits, social proof/testimonial, offer, CTA).
5. **Draft Email Copy:** Have your Agent generate a first draft of the email body copy based on the outline.

6. **Refine and Personalize:** Edit the copy thoroughly. Ensure it aligns with your brand voice, clearly communicates the value, and is persuasive. Add any specific details or personalization touches.
7. **Develop a Clear CTA:** Craft a strong call to action.

Pro-Tip: Consistency and Delivering Genuine Value are Key

Successful email marketing isn't about bombarding subscribers with constant sales pitches. It's about building relationships by consistently delivering genuine value, whether that's through informative content, helpful tips, exclusive insights, or relevant offers. Use your Agent as a partner to help you maintain a regular, engaging, and valuable email schedule that keeps your subscribers looking forward to hearing from you, rather than reaching for the unsubscribe button.

CHAPTER 9

Mastering Social Media Marketing with an AI Agent

Social media is an undeniable force in modern marketing. For small businesses, platforms like Facebook, Instagram, X (formerly Twitter), LinkedIn, Pinterest, and TikTok offer unparalleled opportunities to connect with target audiences, build brand awareness, drive website traffic, and foster customer loyalty. However, navigating the ever-evolving landscape of social media, consistently creating engaging content, and managing multiple platforms can be a significant time drain. This chapter will demonstrate how your Agent can be a strategic partner in your social media marketing efforts, helping you develop content strategies, generate post ideas, craft engaging copy, and even understand performance, all while saving you valuable time and resources.

The Role of Social Media in Your Small Business Marketing Mix

Before leveraging your Agent, it's important to understand the strategic role social media should play for your business. It's not just about accumulating followers; it's about:

- **Building Brand Awareness and Visibility:** Introducing your brand to new potential customers.

- **Engaging with Your Audience:** Creating conversations, answering questions, and building relationships.
- **Driving Website Traffic:** Directing users to your website for more information, lead capture, or sales.
- **Generating Leads:** Using social media to identify and attract potential customers.
- **Showcasing Brand Personality:** Giving your brand a human voice and connecting on a more personal level.
- **Gathering Customer Feedback and Insights:** Listening to what your audience is saying about your brand and industry.
- **Providing Customer Service:** Offering a channel for quick support and issue resolution.

Choosing the right platforms is also crucial. You don't need to be on every social media channel. Focus on the platforms where your target avatar (Chapter 4) spends their time and where your type of content will resonate most effectively.

Developing Your Social Media Content Strategy with Your AI Agent

A successful social media presence requires a clear content strategy. This involves defining your goals for each platform, understanding your audience's content preferences, and planning the types of content you will share. Your Agent can assist in this strategic planning.

- **Brainstorming Content Pillars and Themes:** Content pillars are 3-5 broad topics or themes that your social media content will consistently revolve around, aligned with your brand and your audience's interests. Your Agent can help you brainstorm these pillars based on your business niche, your avatar's pain points and aspirations, and current industry trends.

- **Prompt Example for Your Agent:** "*My small business is a [e.g., 'sustainable fashion boutique for women']. My target avatar, 'Eco-Conscious Emily,' is interested in ethical fashion, styling tips for sustainable pieces, and learning about eco-friendly brands. Brainstorm 4-5 content pillars for my Instagram and Pinterest presence that would resonate with her and align with my brand.*"

- **Creating a Social Media Content Calendar (Conceptual Outline):** While your Agent won't directly populate a calendar tool (yet!), it can help you outline a conceptual content calendar by suggesting a mix of post types (e.g., educational, entertaining, promotional, behind-the-scenes, user-generated content) for each content pillar, and even suggest posting frequencies for different platforms based on common best practices (which you should always test and adapt).

  - **Prompt Example for Your Agent**: "*For the content pillar 'Styling Tips for Sustainable Fashion,' suggest 5 different types of Instagram posts I could create (e.g., carousel showing 3 ways to style one item, a short Reel video, a 'Get the Look' flat lay, a user-generated content feature, a quick tip graphic). Also, suggest a weekly theme idea for this pillar for the next 4 weeks.*"

Generating Engaging Social Media Post Ideas and Copy with Your AI Agent

Coming up with a constant stream of fresh and engaging social media posts is one of the biggest challenges for small businesses. This is where your Agent can truly shine as an idea generator and copywriter's assistant.

- **Brainstorming Post Ideas for Various Platforms:** Provide your Agent with a content pillar, a specific theme, a product you want to highlight, or a current event, and ask it to generate multiple post ideas tailored for different platforms (as the optimal format and tone can vary significantly between, say, LinkedIn and TikTok).
  - **Prompt Example for Your Agent:** "*I want to create social media posts about my new [e.g., 'online course on mindfulness for busy professionals']. Generate 3 post ideas for LinkedIn (focusing on professional benefits and thought leadership), 3 post ideas for Instagram (more visual, perhaps with a quote graphic or a short video tip), and 2 short X (Twitter) post ideas (concise, perhaps with a question to drive engagement).*"
- **Crafting Compelling Captions and Post Copy:** Once you have an idea, your Agent can help you write engaging captions or post copy. You can specify the desired tone (e.g., informative, humorous, inspiring, empathetic), the key message, and any call to action.
  - **Prompt Example for Your Agent**: "*Write an engaging Instagram caption for a photo showcasing a [e.g., 'customer enjoying our new seasonal coffee blend at our cafe']. The tone should be warm and inviting. Mention the*

name of the blend and encourage people to come try it. Include 3-5 relevant hashtags."

- **Generating Questions to Drive Engagement:** Asking questions is a great way to boost comments and interaction on your posts. Your Agent can generate relevant questions related to your content or industry.
- **Writing Ad Copy for Social Media Campaigns:** If you're running paid social media ads, your Agent can help you draft various ad copy options (headlines, body text, CTAs) that you can then A/B test.

Leveraging Your AI Agent for Hashtag Research

Hashtags are crucial for discoverability, especially on platforms like Instagram and X. Using a mix of relevant, popular, niche, and branded hashtags can significantly increase the reach of your posts. Your Agent can assist in brainstorming relevant hashtags.

- **Prompt Example for Your AI Agent:** "*For an Instagram post about [e.g., 'a new vegan recipe for chocolate chip cookies'], generate a list of 15-20 relevant hashtags. Include a mix of broad food hashtags, vegan-specific hashtags, baking hashtags, and some more niche or trending ones if applicable.*"

(Always review AI-generated hashtags to ensure they are genuinely relevant and not associated with inappropriate content.)

Responding to Comments and Messages (Conceptual Assistance)

While your Agent won't directly manage your social media inboxes or comment sections in real-time, it can help you draft thoughtful and appropriate responses to common questions or types of comments if you provide the context.

- **Drafting Template Responses:** For frequently asked questions, your Agent can help you create template responses that you can then quickly personalize and use.
- **Brainstorming Ways to Handle Negative Feedback:** If you receive negative comments, your Agent can help you brainstorm professional and constructive ways to respond, focusing on de-escalation and problem-solving.

Understanding Social Media Analytics (Conceptual Assistance)

Most social media platforms provide built-in analytics tools that offer insights into your audience demographics, post performance (reach, engagement, clicks), and follower growth. While your Agent doesn't directly access these platforms, if you can export key data points (e.g., top-performing posts' topics and formats, engagement rates for different content types) and provide them to the agent in a structured way, it might be able to help you identify patterns or summarize findings.

- **Prompt Example (Conceptual – requires you to provide the data):** "*Based on the following data from my Instagram insights for the last month [e.g., 'Posts about X topic received 50% higher engagement than posts about Y topic. Video posts had twice the reach of static image posts.'], what are 2-3 potential conclusions I can draw to inform my future content strategy?*"

Staying on Top of Trends (with AI Assistance)

Social media trends can change rapidly. Your Agent can help you research current trending topics, challenges, or content formats within your industry or on specific platforms, giving you ideas for timely and relevant content (always ensuring any trend participation aligns with your brand values).

Practical Exercise: Plan and Draft a Week's Worth of Social Media Content for One Platform with Your AI Agent

1. **Choose a Platform and a Content Pillar:** Select one social media platform you want to focus on and one of your key content pillars.
2. **Brainstorm Post Ideas:** Ask your Agent to generate 5-7 post ideas related to that pillar for your chosen platform, aiming for a mix of content types (e.g., tip, question, behind-the-scenes, promotion, user-generated content idea).
3. **Select Your Top Ideas:** Choose 3-4 of the best ideas you'd like to develop for the week.
4. **Draft Post Copy:** For each selected idea, use your Agent to help you draft the caption/post copy. Specify the tone, key message, and any desired call to action.
5. **Generate Hashtags:** For platforms where hashtags are important (like Instagram), ask your Agent to suggest a relevant set of hashtags for each post.
6. **Review and Refine:** Edit all AI-generated copy and hashtag suggestions to ensure they are accurate, on-brand, and engaging. Add your unique voice and any specific details.

7. **Consider Visuals:** For each post, think about what kind of image or video would best accompany the copy. Manus can brainstorm the visual concept for each post and then generate detailed, platform-appropriate prompts for use in image-generation tools like DALL·E or Midjourney. This ensures your visuals align with the message, brand, and tone of the post while streamlining the creative process.

Pro-Tip: Authenticity and Consistency Trump Perfection

While your Agent can help you create polished content, remember that authenticity is key on social media. Let your brand's personality shine through. It's also more important to be consistent with your posting schedule and engagement than to wait for the "perfect" post. Use your Agent to streamline the content creation process so you can focus more on genuine interaction and building relationships with your audience.

CHAPTER 10

SEO Basics for Small Businesses with an AI Agent

Now that your messaging, offers, website and content are dialed in, it's time to make sure customers can actually find you. This is where Search Engine Optimization (SEO) comes into play. SEO is the practice of optimizing your online content so that search engines like Google are more likely to show it as a top result for relevant searches. For small businesses, effective SEO can be a game-changer, driving targeted organic (non-paid) traffic to your website, increasing visibility, and ultimately boosting sales. While SEO can seem complex, this chapter will discuss the fundamentals and demonstrate how your Agent can be a valuable assistant in key SEO tasks, from keyword research to content optimization, helping you lay a solid foundation for getting found online.

SEO Demystified: Why It Matters for Small Business Growth

At its core, SEO is about making your website more attractive to both search engines and users. Search engines aim to provide their users with the most relevant and high-quality results for their queries. By understanding and implementing

SEO best practices, you signal to search engines that your content is valuable and relevant to specific searches.

The benefits of organic traffic generated through SEO are significant:

* **Targeted Audience:** People actively searching for terms related to your products or services are often highly motivated and closer to making a purchase decision.

* **Sustainable Results:** Unlike paid advertising, where traffic stops when you stop paying, well-executed SEO can provide a consistent stream of traffic over the long term.

* **Cost-Effective:** While SEO requires an investment of time and effort (and potentially budget if you hire experts), organic traffic itself is free.

* **Builds Trust and Credibility:** Websites that rank higher in search results are often perceived as more trustworthy and authoritative by users.

Understanding How Search Engines Work (The Basics)

To optimize for search engines, it helps to have a basic understanding of how they operate:

1. **Crawling:** Search engines use automated programs called crawlers (or spiders/bots) to discover new and updated content on the web by following links from one page to another.

2. **Indexing:** Once content is crawled, search engines analyze it (text, images, videos, etc.) and store relevant information in a massive database called an index. This index is like a giant library that the search engine can quickly sift through.

3. **Ranking:** When a user types a query into a search engine, the search engine's algorithm sifts through its index to find the most relevant and high-quality pages and then ranks them in order of perceived relevance and authority on the search engine results page (SERP).

Your Agent can help you understand these concepts in more detail if needed, but this basic framework is sufficient for grasping the fundamentals of SEO.

Keyword Research: Finding the Terms Your Customers Are Searching For with Your AI Agent

Keyword research is the cornerstone of any successful SEO strategy. It involves identifying the specific words and phrases (keywords) that your target audience uses when searching for products, services, or information related to your business. Your Agent can be an excellent brainstorming partner in this process.

Understanding Different Types of Keywords

- **Short-Tail Keywords (or Head Terms):** Broad, general terms, usually 1-2 words (e.g., "coffee," "marketing"). Highly competitive and often have very high search volume.
- **Long-Tail Keywords:** More specific phrases, usually 3+ words (e.g., "best organic coffee beans for french press," "digital marketing services for small retail businesses"). Less competitive, lower individual search volume, but often have higher conversion rates because they indicate more specific intent.

- **Informational Keywords:** Used when people are looking for information (e.g., "how to make cold brew coffee," "what is content marketing").
- **Navigational Keywords:** Used when people are trying to find a specific website or brand (e.g., "Starbucks website," "Manus AI login").
- **Transactional Keywords:** Used when people are looking to make a purchase or take a specific action (e.g., "buy whole bean espresso online," "hire a local plumber").

Brainstorming Seed Keywords

Start by brainstorming a list of "seed" keywords – broad terms directly related to your business, products, and services. Think about how you would describe what you offer.

Using Your AI Agent to Generate Keyword Ideas and Related Terms

Once you have your seed keywords, your Agent can help you expand this list by generating related terms, long-tail variations, and questions your audience might be asking.

- **Prompt Example for Your AI Agent:** "*My small business offers [e.g., 'handmade leather journals']. My target customers are writers, artists, and people who appreciate unique, handcrafted gifts. Generate a list of 30 potential keywords, including a mix of short-tail and long-tail variations, that these customers might use when searching for products like mine. Also, suggest 5 informational keywords related to journaling or leather craft.*"

Analyzing Keyword Intent and Relevance

For each keyword idea, consider the user's intent behind the search. Are they looking to learn, compare, or buy? Ensure the keywords you target are highly relevant to the content you can provide and the solutions your business offers. Your Agent can help you think through the potential intent behind different keyword phrases.

(Note: While your Agent is excellent for generating keyword ideas and understanding concepts, for detailed metrics like search volume, keyword difficulty, and competitor keyword analysis, you would typically use dedicated SEO tools like Google Keyword Planner, Ahrefs, SEMrush, Moz Keyword Explorer, or Keywords Everywhere. Your Agent can help you interpret the data from these tools and turn insights into action.)

On-Page SEO: Optimizing Your Website Content with Your AI Agent

On-page SEO refers to optimizing the elements directly within your website pages to improve their ranking and visibility. Your Agent can be particularly helpful in crafting SEO-friendly content.

Crafting SEO-Friendly Page Titles and Meta Descriptions

- **Page Titles (Title Tags):** The clickable headline that appears in search results and browser tabs. It should be concise (typically 50-60 characters), accurately describe the page content, and include your primary target keyword for that page.

- **Meta Descriptions:** The short snippet of text (around 150-160 characters) that appears below the page title in search results. While not a direct ranking factor, a compelling meta description can significantly influence click-through rates by enticing users to visit your page. It should summarize the page content and include relevant keywords.
- **Prompt Example for Your Agent:** "*Write an SEO-friendly page title (under 60 characters) and a compelling meta description (under 160 characters) for a webpage about my [e.g., 'dog grooming services in Springfield, IL']. The primary keyword for this page is 'dog grooming Springfield IL.' The page details our services, pricing, and our gentle approach.*"

Writing High-Quality, Keyword-Rich Content

As discussed in Chapter 6 (Website Crafting) and Chapter 8 (Content Creation – which will be the next chapter), creating valuable, informative, and engaging content is paramount. For SEO, this content should also naturally incorporate your target keywords. Your Agent can help you draft blog posts, service pages, and other website content that is both user-friendly and optimized for relevant keywords. Avoid "keyword stuffing" (unnaturally cramming keywords into your content), as this can harm your rankings and user experience. Focus on creating content that genuinely answers the user's query related to the keyword.

Optimizing Header Tags (H1, H2, H3, etc.)

Optimizing Header Tags (H1, H2, H3, etc.)

Header tags (<h1>, <h2>, <h3>, etc.) help structure your content for readability and signal to search engines the hierarchy and topics of your page. Your main page title should typically be an <h1> tag and include your primary keyword. Subheadings (<h2>, <h3>) should break up your content and can incorporate secondary or related keywords.

Image ***SEO***: Writing Descriptive Alt Text

Alternative text (alt text) is a description of an image that appears if the image fails to load and is also read by screen readers for visually impaired users. Search engines also use alt text to understand the content of an image. Your alt text should be concise, descriptive, and can include relevant keywords if appropriate. If you describe an image to your Agent, it can help you draft suitable alt text.

- **Prompt Example for Your Agent:** "*I have an image on my website showing [e.g., 'a golden retriever puppy happily playing with a red ball in a grassy park']. Write a concise and descriptive alt text for this image that could also be beneficial for SEO if the page is about puppy training tips.*"

Internal Linking Strategies

Internal links are links from one page on your website to another page on your own website. They help users navigate your site, distribute "link equity" (ranking power) throughout your site, and help search engines understand the relationship between your content. When creating new content, think about relevant existing pages you can link to, using descriptive anchor text (the clickable text of the link).

For example, if you're writing a blog post on "10 Healthy Morning Habits," and you've previously published a guide on "Easy 10-Minute Workouts," you might include a sentence like: "Pair these habits with an easy 10-minute workout to boost your energy all day."

Local SEO: Winning in Your Neighborhood with Your AI Agent

For small businesses with a physical location or those that serve a specific geographic area (e.g., plumbers, restaurants, local retail stores), Local SEO is critical. It focuses on optimizing your online presence to attract more customers from relevant local searches.

The Importance of Local Search

Many searches have local intent (e.g., "pizza near me," "best coffee shop in downtown"). Appearing in these local search results, often displayed in a "map pack" or local listing, can drive significant foot traffic and calls.

Optimizing Your Google Business Profile (GBP)

Google Business Profile (formerly Google My Business) is a free tool that allows you to manage how your business appears on Google Search and Maps. It's one of the most important elements of Local SEO. Ensure your GBP listing is complete, accurate, and regularly updated. Your Agent can help you draft various sections of your GBP:

* **Business Description:** A compelling overview of your business. * **Services/Products:** Detailed lists of what you offer.

* **Posts:** Regular updates (like mini-blog posts or announcements) to keep your profile fresh.

* **Responding to Reviews:** Crafting thoughtful responses to both positive and negative reviews. * **Answering Questions:** Providing answers to questions potential customers ask on your profile.

- **Prompt Example for Your Agent:** "*Help me draft a compelling business description (around 750 characters) for my Google Business Profile. My business is a [e.g., 'family-owned Italian restaurant in Boise, Idaho, known for authentic pasta dishes and a cozy atmosphere']. Highlight our key features and what makes us unique.*"

Building Local Citations (NAP Consistency)

A citation is any online mention of your business's Name, Address, and Phone number (NAP). Consistency of this NAP information across various online directories (like Yelp, Yellow Pages, local chamber of commerce sites, industry-specific directories) is crucial for Local SEO. While your Agent can't build these citations for you, it can help you research relevant local directories where your business should be listed.

Encouraging and Managing Online Reviews

Online reviews (on Google, Yelp, Facebook, etc.) are a significant factor in Local SEO and heavily influence customer decisions. Encourage satisfied customers to leave reviews. Monitor and respond to all reviews professionally. Your Agent can help you draft polite requests for reviews or responses to existing ones.

Practical Exercise: Optimize a Piece of Content for a Target Keyword with Your Agent

1. **Choose a Piece of Content:** Select an existing blog post or website page (or plan a new one).
2. **Identify a Primary Keyword:** If you haven't already, use your Agent to help you brainstorm and select a primary target keyword for this piece of content.

3. **Draft/Review Page Title and Meta Description:** Use your Agent to help you craft an SEO-friendly page title and meta description incorporating the keyword.
4. **Analyze Content for Keyword Integration:** Review the main body content. Does it naturally incorporate the primary keyword and related terms? If not, ask your Agent for suggestions on how to weave them in organically while maintaining readability and value.
5. **Check Header Tags:** Ensure your main heading is an H1 and uses the primary keyword. Use H2s and H3s for subtopics.
6. **Optimize Images:** If there are images, describe them to your Agent and ask for help drafting descriptive alt text.

Pro-Tip: SEO is a Marathon, Not a Sprint

SEO takes time and consistent effort to show results. Don't get discouraged if you don't see top rankings overnight. Focus on consistently creating high-quality, user-focused content, optimizing it based on sound SEO principles (with your Agent's help for brainstorming and drafting), and building a positive online reputation. Your Agent can be a valuable long-term partner in this ongoing process.

Recommendation:

For an affordable one stop shop solution to your SEO needs, I highly recommend Search Atlas and OTTO – the first automated AI assistant. It automates technical fixes, content optimizations, backlink building, and content creation in just a few clicks.

CHAPTER 11

Content Creation King: Generating High-Quality Marketing Content with an AI Agent

In the digital marketing realm, content is not just king; it is the entire kingdom. High-quality, relevant, and engaging content is what attracts your audience, builds trust, educates potential customers, and ultimately drives conversions. For small businesses, however, the demand for a consistent stream of diverse content – from blog posts and website copy to social media updates, email newsletters, and video scripts – can be relentless and overwhelming. This is where your Agent transforms from a helpful assistant into a veritable content creation powerhouse. This chapter shows you the myriad ways your Agent can help you generate various forms of high-quality marketing content, streamline your content production process, and maintain a strong, consistent brand voice across all your channels.

The Strategic Importance of High-Quality Content

Before diving into how your Agent can assist, let's underscore why high-quality content is so vital:

- **Attracts and Engages Your Target Audience:** Valuable content draws in potential customers who are actively seeking solutions or information that your business provides.

- **Builds Authority and Trust:** Consistently providing insightful and helpful content positions your business as an expert and a trusted resource in your industry.
- **Supports SEO Efforts:** Well-optimized content is crucial for improving your website's visibility in search engine results (as discussed in Chapter 8).
- **Nurtures Leads:** Content can guide potential customers through the buyer's journey, from initial awareness to consideration and decision.
- **Drives Conversions:** Compelling content, combined with clear calls to action, can directly lead to sales, sign-ups, or other desired outcomes.
- **Fosters Customer Loyalty:** Ongoing valuable content keeps your existing customers engaged and reinforces their decision to choose your brand.

Your Agent as a Versatile Content Writing Partner

Your Agent's ability to process information and generate human-like text makes it an incredibly versatile partner for various content writing tasks. Remember, the goal is to use the Agent as a co-creator; it generates drafts and ideas, and you provide the strategic direction, industry expertise, brand voice refinement, and final polish.

Crafting Engaging Blog Posts and Articles

Blogs are excellent for SEO, thought leadership, and providing in-depth value to your audience. Your Agent can assist in every stage of blog post creation:

- **Brainstorming Blog Post Topics:** (Referencing Chapter 5 on idea generation) Your Agent can generate a wealth of topic ideas based on your industry, target avatar, and keywords.
- **Creating Detailed Outlines:** Once you have a topic, your Agent can help you structure the blog post by creating a logical outline with key sections and subheadings.
  - **Prompt Example for Your Agent:** "*Create a detailed blog post outline for the topic 'The Top 5 Benefits of Using Organic Skincare Products.' The target audience is health-conscious consumers aged 25-45. The outline should include an introduction, five main benefit sections with points to cover in each, and a conclusion with a call to action to explore our product line.*"
- **Drafting Initial Content:** Your Agent can write a first draft of the blog post based on the outline and any specific information or keywords you provide. This can save you significant time.
  - **Prompt Example for Your Agent:** "*Using the outline provided [or refer to a previous outline], write a first draft of a 1000-word blog post on 'The Top 5 Benefits of Using Organic Skincare Products.' Maintain an informative and slightly persuasive tone. Incorporate the keywords 'organic skincare benefits' and 'natural beauty products' naturally throughout the text.*"

Developing Compelling Website Copy

As covered in Chapter 6, your Agent can help generate copy for all key pages of your website, including homepages, about pages, service/product descriptions, and FAQs. The focus here is on ensuring the copy is not only informative but also persuasive and aligned with your brand's voice.

Writing Persuasive Email Marketing Copy

Chapter 7 detailed how your Agent can assist in crafting email subject lines, welcome sequences, promotional emails, and newsletters. The key is to provide the Agent with clear objectives for each email and information about the target segment.

Generating Engaging Social Media Content

As discussed in Chapter 8, your Agent can help brainstorm post ideas, write captions, generate questions, and even suggest relevant hashtags for various social media platforms, tailoring the content to the specific nuances of each channel.

Expanding Beyond Text: Your AI Agent for Multimedia Content Ideas and Scripts

Content is not limited to the written word. Video, audio (podcasts), and visual content are increasingly important for engaging audiences. While your Agent may not directly create the final multimedia files, it can be invaluable in the planning and scripting stages. As of this writing, Manus is just beginning to make images and can create full power point presentations. These functions will improve significantly in a very short time.

Outlining Video Scripts

Video content, whether for YouTube, social media, or your website (e.g., product demos, tutorials, customer testimonials, vlogs), requires a script or at least a detailed outline. Your

Agent can help you structure your video content for maximum impact.

- **Prompt Example for Your Agent:** "*Create a 2-minute video script outline for a product demonstration of my [e.g., 'new smart home coffee maker']. The script should have three main parts: 1. Introduction to the problem it solves (e.g., inconsistent coffee). 2. Demonstration of 3 key features and their benefits. 3. A clear call to action to visit our website to learn more or purchase. Suggest visuals for each part.*"

Generating Podcast Episode Ideas and Outlines

If podcasting is part of your content strategy, your Agent can help you brainstorm episode topics relevant to your audience, create outlines for solo shows or interview questions for guests, and even draft introductory or concluding scripts.

- **Prompt Example for Your Agent:** "*I host a podcast for [e.g., 'freelance graphic designers']. Generate 5 podcast episode ideas that would provide actionable advice or inspiration for this audience. For one of those ideas, 'Pricing Your Design Services Effectively,' create a brief episode outline with 3-4 key discussion points.*"

Repurposing Content with Your AI Agent: Getting More Mileage from Your Efforts

Creating high-quality content takes time and effort. Repurposing existing content into different formats allows you to reach a wider audience and get more value from your initial investment. Your Agent can be a fantastic assistant in this process.

Examples of repurposing include:

* Turning a detailed blog post into a series of social media updates, an infographic summary, a short video script, or an email newsletter segment.

* Expanding a popular social media post into a more in-depth blog article.

* Transcribing a video or podcast and using the text to create blog posts or articles (your Agent can help summarize or reformat transcribed text).

- **Prompt Example for Your Agent:** "*I have a blog post titled '10 Time-Management Tips for Busy Entrepreneurs' [you could paste the text or a detailed summary]. Repurpose this content into:*

1. Five engaging tweets, each highlighting one or two tips.

2. A short Facebook post summarizing the key takeaways.

3. An outline for a 3-minute explainer video."

Remember to review and edit all the generated content to ensure it perfectly aligns with your nuanced brand voice and specific messaging goals.

Practical Exercise: Create a Piece of Content with Your Agent (From Ideation to Draft)

1. **Choose a Content Type and Goal:** Decide on a piece of content you need (e.g., a blog post to drive organic traffic, a social media campaign to announce a new product, an email to nurture leads).
2. **Define Your Audience and Key Message:** Who are you trying to reach? What is the single most important thing you want to communicate?

3. **Brainstorm with Your Agent:** Use prompts to generate topic ideas, angles, or campaign concepts.
4. **Outline with Your Agent:** Once you have a core idea, ask your Agent to help you create a detailed outline or structure for the content.
5. **Draft with Your Agent:** Provide the outline and any other relevant information (keywords, brand voice guidelines, desired length) to your Agent and ask it to generate a first draft.
6. **Review, Edit, and Personalize:** This is the crucial human step. Read through the AI-generated draft critically.
   - Fact-check all information.
   - Refine the language to perfectly match your brand voice.
   - Add your unique insights, examples, anecdotes, and personality.
   - Ensure the content flows well and is engaging for your target audience.
   - Check for any awkward phrasing or repetition.

Pro-Tip: Your AI Agent is an Assistant, You Are the Editor-in-Chief

Think of your Agent as a highly efficient junior writer or research assistant. It can produce a large volume of work and generate excellent starting points, but it lacks your deep industry knowledge, your specific business context, your understanding of your customers' nuances, and your unique creative vision. Always be prepared to guide, edit, and refine the AI-generated content to ensure it meets your quality standards and truly represents your brand. The combination of AI efficiency and human expertise is what leads to truly exceptional content.

CHAPTER 12

Streamlining Your Marketing Workflow with an AI Agent

In the fast-paced world of small business, time is often your most precious commodity. Marketing, while crucial, can consume a significant portion of this valuable resource. From managing social media to crafting email campaigns and analyzing results, the list of tasks can seem endless. This chapter discusses how your Agent can become an indispensable ally in streamlining your marketing workflow, automating repetitive tasks, and freeing you up to focus on strategy, creativity, and customer relationships. By leveraging AI, you can transform your marketing operations from a time-consuming chore into an efficient, data-driven engine for growth.

The Power of Automation and Efficiency in Marketing

Marketing automation involves using software and technology to execute repetitive marketing tasks, nurture leads, and personalize customer experiences. For small businesses, this can be a game-changer:

- **Time Savings:** Automating tasks like email scheduling, social media posting, and basic customer service inquiries frees up significant time.

- **Increased Efficiency:** AI can handle large volumes of data and execute tasks much faster than a human, leading to more being done with less.
- **Improved Consistency:** Automated processes ensure that your messaging and branding are consistent across all touchpoints.
- **Better Lead Nurturing:** Automated follow-up sequences can nurture leads through the sales funnel more effectively.
- **Enhanced Personalization:** AI can help analyze customer data to deliver more personalized marketing messages at scale.
- **Data-Driven Insights:** AI tools can quickly analyze campaign performance, providing actionable insights for optimization.

Your Agent, while not a dedicated marketing automation platform itself, can be instrumental in many of the *processes* that feed into and support these automated systems, as well as directly handling certain tasks.

Identifying Repetitive Marketing Tasks for AI Assistance

The first step to streamlining your workflow is identifying tasks that are repetitive, time-consuming, and can be effectively handled or assisted by your Agent. Consider these areas:

- **Content Generation (First Drafts):** As discussed in Chapter 9, your Agent can draft blog posts, social media updates, email copy, and ad creatives.
- **Market Research Summarization:** Condensing long reports or articles into key takeaways (Chapter 2).

- **Customer Service FAQs:** Drafting responses to frequently asked questions.
- **Social Media Scheduling (Conceptual Planning):** While the AI might not directly post, it can help you plan a content calendar and draft posts in advance.
- **Data Entry and Organization (Conceptual):** If you can describe a data organization task, the AI might be able to suggest ways to structure it or even generate scripts for simple data manipulation if you provide the data in a text format.
- **Competitor Monitoring (Basic):** Periodically asking your Agent to search for recent news or updates about your key competitors.

Using Your AI Agent for Content Scheduling and Calendar Management (Conceptual)

While your Agent doesn't directly integrate with scheduling tools, it can be a powerful assistant in the planning and content creation phase that precedes scheduling.

- **Brainstorming a Content Calendar:** You can ask your Agent to help you generate ideas for a month's worth of social media posts or blog topics based on specific themes, upcoming holidays, or industry events.
  - **Prompt Example for Your Agent:** "*My small business is a [e.g., 'local bakery']. Next month is [e.g., 'October'], which includes Halloween. Help me brainstorm a content calendar for my Instagram account for October. I want to focus on seasonal specials, behind-the-scenes baking, and customer engagement. Suggest 4 weekly themes and 3-4 post ideas for each theme.*"

- **Generating Content for Scheduled Posts:** Once you have your calendar, you can use the Agent to draft the copy for each post, create image suggestions (which you would then create or source), or outline video scripts.

Automating Customer Interaction (Initial Triage and FAQs)

Your Agent can be programmed (conceptually, or through integration with chatbot platforms if you have that capability) to handle initial customer inquiries or direct them to the right resources.

- **Drafting Standard Responses:** For common questions received via email or social media (e.g., about business hours, product availability, return policies), your Agent can help you draft clear and concise standard responses that you can quickly adapt and send.
- **Creating FAQ Pages:** As mentioned in Chapter 6, your Agent can help generate comprehensive FAQ sections for your website, which can reduce the number of repetitive inquiries.

Streamlining Reporting and Analytics (Data Interpretation Assistance)

Most marketing platforms (social media, email marketing, website analytics) provide a wealth of data. Understanding this data is key to optimizing your efforts. While your Agent cannot directly access your private analytics dashboards, you can feed it summarized data or specific reports and ask for help in interpreting it or identifying trends.

- **Summarizing Performance Reports:** If you export a report (e.g., a social media engagement report or an email campaign performance summary) into a text format, you could ask your Agent to summarize the key findings or identify the best-performing content types.
  - **Prompt Example for Your Agent:** "*I have the following data from my last email campaign: Open Rate - 25%, Click-Through Rate - 5%, Conversion Rate - 1%, Unsubscribe Rate - 0.5%. The campaign promoted [product/ service]. What are some general insights or areas I might want to investigate further based on these metrics?*" (Note: The AI's response will be general without more context, but it can point you in directions to explore).
- **Identifying Trends in Customer Feedback:** If you collect customer feedback (e.g., from surveys or online reviews) and provide it to your Agent, it can help you identify recurring themes, positive points, and areas for improvement.

Integrating Manus with Other Tools (Conceptual)

While Manus, as an Agent, might not have direct API integrations with every marketing tool you use, think about how you can use it as a central "brain" to process information and generate content that can then be fed into other systems.

- **Content Creation for Different Platforms:** Generate a blog post with Manus, then ask it to help you create a shorter version for LinkedIn, a series of tweets, and a visual idea for Instagram based on that same core content.

- **Idea Generation for A/B Testing:** Use Manus to brainstorm different headlines for an email campaign or different calls to action for a landing page, which you then implement and test using your existing marketing platforms.

Practical Exercise: Automate a Repetitive Research Task

1. **Identify a Repetitive Research Task:** Think about a piece of information you regularly need to look up for your marketing (e.g., trending topics in your industry, competitor activities, popular hashtags for a specific theme).
2. **Formulate a Standard Prompt:** Create a clear, concise prompt that you can regularly give to your Agent to perform this research.
3. **Schedule a Reminder:** Set a recurring reminder for yourself (e.g., weekly) to run this prompt with your Agent.
4. **Process and Utilize the Information:** Use the information gathered by your Agent to inform your content strategy, social media posts, or other marketing decisions.

Pro-Tip: Start Small and Iterate

Don't try to automate everything at once. Start by identifying one or two key areas where your Agent can save you the most time or provide the most value. As you become more comfortable working with your Agent, you can gradually expand its role in your marketing workflow. Regularly evaluate what's working and what's not, and refine your prompts and processes for continuous improvement.

By strategically leveraging your Agent to handle repetitive tasks and provide data-driven insights, you can free up your time and mental energy to focus on the high-level strategy, creative thinking, and personal connections that truly drive small business success.

CHAPTER 13

Getting Started with Your AI Agent: Project Setup, Permissions, and Secure Collaboration

Throughout this book, we've explored the vast potential of your Agent to revolutionize your small business marketing. From deep market research and crafting compelling content to streamlining workflows, your AI partner can significantly amplify your efforts. However, to unlock its full capabilities, especially for tasks that involve accessing external websites or platforms, it's crucial to understand how to set up projects effectively and manage permissions and login information securely. This chapter provides practical guidance on initiating projects with your Agent, navigating the sensitive area of credentials, and establishing best practices for a secure and productive human-AI collaboration.

Defining Your Marketing Project: Clarity is Key

Before you even begin a task with your Agent, a clear project definition is essential. This is akin to creating a good brief for a human team member. The more clarity you provide upfront, the more efficiently and effectively your Agent can work.

Key elements to define for any marketing project include:

- **Objective:** What is the primary goal of this project? (e.g., "Increase website traffic by 20% in the next quarter," "Launch a new product successfully," "Improve social media engagement on Instagram.")
- **Scope:** What specific tasks are involved? What are the deliverables? What is explicitly *out* of scope?
- **Target Audience:** Who are you trying to reach with this project? (Refer to your customer avatars from Chapter 4).
- **Key Information & Resources:** What existing information, data, brand guidelines, or access credentials will the Agent need? (We'll cover secure credential handling shortly).
- **Timeline:** Are there any deadlines or key milestones?
- **Metrics for Success:** How will you measure the success of this project?

Documenting these elements, even briefly, will help you structure your requests to the Agent and ensure you both are working towards the same outcome.

Initiating a Project with Your AI Agent: The First Conversation

Think of starting a new project with your Agent like an initial briefing meeting. You need to provide context and clear instructions.

1. **State the Overall Project Goal:** Begin by telling your Agent the main objective of the project.

- *Example:* "Agent, I want to start a project to improve the SEO of my small business website, [yourwebsite.com]. The goal is to increase organic search traffic over the next three months."

2. **Break Down Initial Tasks:** Outline the first few tasks you want the Agent to undertake.

   - *Example (Continuing from above):* "To start, I need your help with comprehensive keyword research for my main services: [list services]. Then, I want you to help me optimize the page titles and meta descriptions for my top 5 service pages."

3. **Provide Necessary Context and Information:** Share any relevant background information, links to your website, information about your target audience, or existing research you've done.

The Sensitive Topic: Managing Permissions and Logins Securely

Many advanced marketing tasks may require your Agent to interact with external websites or platforms on your behalf. This could include:

- Accessing your website's content management system (CMS) to help update content (conceptually, by providing you with the content to paste).
- Monitoring competitor websites for changes.
- Gathering data from specific online sources that might require a login (e.g., private forums, specific analytics tools if you can provide data exports).

- Assisting with social media content planning (though direct posting is usually handled by dedicated social media management tools).

This is where the issue of permissions and login credentials becomes critical. **Directly sharing your primary login credentials (usernames and passwords) with any third party, including an Agent, carries inherent security risks and is generally not recommended as a first resort.**

Best Practices for Secure Collaboration and Access:

1. **Prioritize Agent's Built-in Capabilities:** First, explore if the task can be accomplished using the Agent's inherent capabilities without needing direct external access. For example, for website content updates, the AI can generate the content, and you can manually copy and paste it into your CMS.
2. **Use Dedicated or Limited-Access Accounts (If Possible):** If a platform allows for the creation of secondary user accounts with restricted permissions (e.g., a "viewer" or "editor" role rather than full "administrator"), consider creating such an account specifically for tasks where AI assistance is needed. This limits potential exposure if the account were compromised.
3. **Temporary Access & Immediate Revocation:** If you must provide access using a specific account, and the platform supports it, consider changing the password temporarily for the duration of the task and then changing it back immediately afterward. Revoke any temporary access as soon as the task is complete.

4. **The Agent's Secure Environment (If Applicable):** Understand the security measures your specific Agent platform has in place. Reputable Agent systems operate within secure sandbox environments designed to protect data. However, this doesn't negate your responsibility for careful credential management.

5. **Manual Intervention for Sensitive Actions (The Safest Route):** For highly sensitive actions (e.g., making purchases, accessing financial information, making critical changes to live systems), the safest approach is often for the Agent to guide *you* through the process or prepare the necessary information, and then *you* perform the action manually by logging into the platform yourself. Your Agent can tell you what steps to take, what information to input, or what to look for, but you are the one interacting directly with the sensitive platform.

   – *Example:* If your Agent helps you draft ad copy for a social media campaign, you would then log into your social media ads manager yourself to set up and launch the campaign using the AI-generated copy.

6. **Consider Browser Takeover (If Offered and Appropriate):** Some Agent systems might offer a feature where you can temporarily grant the agent control of your browser session to perform specific actions on a website *while you are supervising.* This can be useful for tasks like filling out forms or navigating complex sites. However, only use this feature if you fully trust the Agent platform, understand the implications, and are actively monitoring the session.

7. Always log out of sensitive accounts after such a session. (Manus supports browser takeover. When needed, the AI will send a message explicitly suggesting browser takeover with specific instructions, and you can choose to either complete the task yourself or provide alternative information through conversation).
8. **Regularly Review Account Activity:** If you do grant any form of access, regularly monitor the activity on those accounts for any unauthorized actions.
9. **Use Strong, Unique Passwords and Two-Factor Authentication (2FA):** This is a general security best practice but is especially important for any accounts your Agent might interact with, even indirectly. Ensure 2FA is enabled wherever possible.

Communicating About Logins with Your AI Agent:

If, after considering all alternatives, you determine that providing some form of access is necessary and you've taken steps to minimize risk (e.g., using a temporary or restricted account):

- **Be Explicit and Cautious:** Clearly state which platform the credentials are for.
- **Provide Only What's Necessary:** Don't share more information than is absolutely required for the task.
- **Confirm Deletion/Forgetting (If Applicable):** If the Agent's platform has a mechanism for "forgetting" information, use it after the task is complete. However, assume that any information shared could potentially be logged, which underscores the importance of temporary or restricted credentials.

A Note on Trust and Responsibility: While Agents are designed to be helpful, the ultimate responsibility for the security of your accounts and data lies with you. Always err on the side of caution.

Setting Up for Specific Project Types:

Let's consider how you might approach setup for common marketing projects involving your Agent:

Project: Website Content Overhaul

- **Objective:** Update all service pages and the About Us page with new, SEO-optimized copy.
- **Agent's Role:** Keyword research, drafting new copy, suggesting internal linking opportunities.
- **Permissions/Logins:** Likely none directly needed by the AI. It generates content, you review and upload it to your website CMS.

Project: Competitor Monitoring

- **Objective:** Track key competitors' new blog posts and social media announcements weekly.
- **Agent's Role:** Perform web searches for "[Competitor Name] blog" or "[Competitor Name] news" and summarize findings.
- **Permissions/Logins:** None needed. The AI uses its public web browsing capabilities.

Project: Social Media Content Calendar Creation

- **Objective:** Develop a one-month content calendar for Instagram, including post ideas, captions, and hashtag suggestions.

- **Agent's Role:** Brainstorm themes, generate post ideas, draft captions, research hashtags.
- **Permissions/Logins:** None needed by the AI for content creation. You would use a separate social media scheduling tool to post the content.

Working Effectively: Iteration and Feedback

Once a project is underway, effective collaboration with your Agent involves:

- **Clear Prompts:** (More on this in Chapter 13) Provide specific instructions for each task.
- **Iterative Refinement:** The AI's first output may not be perfect. Provide feedback and ask for revisions.
- **Breaking Down Complex Tasks:** Divide large projects into smaller, manageable steps.
- **Saving Your Work:** Keep records of important outputs, prompts, and project decisions.

Practical Exercise: Plan a Small Marketing Project with AI Assistance

1. **Choose a Small, Manageable Project:** (e.g., "Write 3 blog posts on X topic," "Research 5 potential influencers in Y niche," "Draft a welcome email sequence.")
2. **Define Project Elements:** Briefly outline the objective, scope, target audience, and any key information for your Agent.
3. **Identify Necessary Resources/Access:** Determine if any external website access would be *conceptually* helpful. Then, decide on the safest way to achieve the

goal (e.g., AI provides information, you perform actions; AI uses public web access only).

4. **Draft Your Initial Prompt(s):** Write down the first few instructions you would give to your Agent to kick off this project.

Pro-Tip: Establish a Secure Routine

Develop a consistent and secure routine for any tasks that might involve your Agent interacting with external information or requiring you to log into platforms based on its guidance. Always prioritize security and be mindful of the information you share and how access is managed. Your Agent is a powerful tool, and like any powerful tool, it should be used responsibly and with appropriate safeguards.

CHAPTER 14

Mastering Prompts: How to Talk to Your AI Agent for Maximum Marketing Impact

As we've seen in previous chapters, your Agent, Manus, can be an incredibly powerful tool for a vast array of marketing tasks. However, the quality of the output you receive from Manus is directly proportional to the quality of the input you provide. In the world of AI, this input often comes in the form of "prompts." Mastering the art of crafting effective prompts is akin to learning how to communicate clearly and precisely with a highly intelligent assistant. This chapter will discuss the principles of effective prompt engineering, providing you with the techniques to unlock Manus's full potential and get the exact results you need for your small business marketing efforts.

Understanding the Correct Way To Prompt Manus

As we've seen in previous chapters, your Agent, Manus, can be an incredibly powerful tool for a vast array of marketing tasks. However, the quality of the output you receive from Manus is directly proportional to the quality of the input you provide. In the world of AI, this input often comes in the form of "prompts." Mastering the art of crafting effective prompts is akin to learning how to communicate clearly and precisely with a highly intelligent assistant. This chapter will discuss into the principles of effective prompt engineering, providing you with the techniques to unlock Manus's full potential and get the exact results you need for your small business marketing efforts.

Understanding the "Why" Behind Effective Prompts

Think of your Agent as an incredibly knowledgeable and capable entity, but one that relies entirely on your instructions to understand what you want it to do. A vague or poorly constructed prompt will likely lead to generic, irrelevant, or unhelpful responses. Conversely, a well-crafted prompt acts as a precise set of instructions, guiding the AI to deliver targeted, high-quality output that meets your specific needs.

Effective prompting helps you to:

- **Get More Relevant Results:** Clearly defining your request ensures the AI focuses on the right topic and delivers information pertinent to your specific context.
- **Improve Output Quality:** Providing sufficient detail and context helps the AI generate more accurate, coherent, and useful responses.
- **Save Time and Effort:** Well-crafted prompts reduce the need for multiple iterations and extensive editing, making your workflow more efficient.
- **Unlock Advanced Capabilities:** Sophisticated prompts can tap into the AI's deeper reasoning and creative generation abilities.

Core Principles of Effective Prompt Engineering

While prompting can be an iterative process of trial and error, several core principles can significantly improve your success rate from the outset.

1. **Be Specific and Clear:** Avoid ambiguity. The more precise your language, the better the AI will understand your intent. Instead of saying, "Write about my product," say, "Write a 500-word blog post explaining the top 3 benefits of my eco-friendly coffee beans for environmentally conscious consumers aged 25-40."
2. **Provide Sufficient Context:** The AI doesn't inherently know your business, your brand voice, your target audience, or your specific goals unless you tell it. Provide relevant background information to help it tailor its response.
   - *Examples of Context:* Your industry, your target customer avatar (referencing Chapter 4), your brand's tone of voice (e.g., professional, friendly, witty), the specific goal of the content you're requesting, any key information or data points to include.
3. **Define the Desired Output Format:** Tell the AI what kind of output you expect. Do you want a bulleted list, a paragraph, a blog post outline, a table, a script, a piece of code, or a summary? Specifying the format helps the AI structure its response appropriately.
   - **Prompt Example:** "*Generate a bulleted list of 5 potential taglines for a new artisanal bakery specializing in sourdough bread.*" vs. "*Write a short paragraph*

describing the unique qualities of artisanal sourdough bread."

4. **Assign a Role or Persona (Optional but Powerful):** You can instruct the AI to adopt a specific persona or role, which can significantly influence the tone, style, and perspective of its output. This is particularly useful for marketing content.
   - **Prompt Example:** "*Act as an experienced marketing consultant advising a small business owner. Explain the importance of defining a target audience in simple terms.*" or "*Write a product description for a new gaming mouse from the perspective of an enthusiastic professional gamer.*"
5. **Specify Constraints and Requirements:** If there are any limitations or specific requirements, include them in your prompt. This could be word count, character limits (for social media or meta descriptions), keywords to include, information to exclude, or a specific call to action.
   - **Prompt Example***:* "*Draft three different Facebook ad headlines for our upcoming webinar on 'Small Business Cybersecurity.' Each headline must be under 10 words and include the phrase 'Free Webinar.'*"
6. **Use Examples (Few-Shot Prompting):** If you have a specific style or format in mind, providing one or two examples within your prompt (known as few-shot prompting) can be incredibly effective in guiding the AI to produce similar output.
   - **Prompt Example:** "*I need to write short, catchy product descriptions. Here are a couple of examples: Example 1: 'Product A: Handcrafted leather wallet. Timeless style, built to last.' Example 2: 'Product B:*

Organic herbal tea. Soothe your senses, naturally.' Now, write a similar short, catchy product description for: 'Product C: Eco-friendly bamboo toothbrush."

7. **Break Down Complex Tasks:** For complicated requests, it's often better to break them down into a series of smaller, more manageable prompts. This allows you to guide the AI step-by-step and refine the output at each stage.

   – **Example:** Instead of asking the AI to write an entire marketing plan in one go, you might first ask it to help research the target market, then brainstorm campaign ideas, then draft copy for specific elements, and so on.

8. **Iterate and Refine:** Don't expect the first response to always be perfect. Prompting is often an iterative process. If the initial output isn't quite right, analyze what went wrong and refine your prompt. You can ask the AI to elaborate, simplify, change the tone, or focus on a different aspect.

   – **Follow-up Prompt Example:** "*That's a good start, but can you make the tone more enthusiastic and add a stronger call to action at the end?*"

Prompt Structures and Techniques for Marketing Tasks

Let's look at some common prompt structures and techniques tailored for specific marketing tasks discussed in this book:

For Market Research (Chapter 3):

- **Structure:** "*Research and summarize [specific topic/data point] related to [industry/market]. Focus on [specific aspects,* *e.g., trends, statistics, competitor actions]. Provide sources if possible."*

- **Technique:** Be specific about the type of information and the desired level of detail.

For Customer Avatar Creation (Chapter 4):

- **Structure:** "*Based on the following information [provide research data/observations], draft a customer avatar profile for a [type of business] targeting [audience segment]. Include sections for [demographics, goals, pain points, values, etc.]. Give the avatar a name: [Name].*"
- **Technique:** Provide as much raw data or context about the target audience as possible.

For Idea Generation (Chapter 5):

- **Structure:** "*Brainstorm [number] unique [type of ideas, e.g., marketing campaign ideas, blog post titles, product names] for a [type of business/ product] targeting [specific avatar/ audience]. The ideas should be [desired characteristic, e.g., innovative, budget-friendly, humorous].*"
- **Technique:** Encourage creativity by asking for "unique" or "unconventional" ideas or by setting constraints that force novel thinking.

For Content Creation (Chapter 9):

- **Structure (Blog Post Draft):** "*Act as a [e.g., 'seasoned travel writer']. Write a first draft of a [word count] blog post titled '[Title]' based on the following outline [provide outline]. The tone should be [e.g., 'adventurous and inspiring']. Incorporate the keywords [list keywords] naturally. Include a call to action to [desired action].*"

- **Structure (Social Media Caption):** "*Write an engaging Instagram caption for an image showing [describe image]. The tone should be [e.g., 'playful and witty']. Include [number] relevant hashtags and a question to encourage comments.*"
- **Technique:** Be very clear about the desired tone, length, keywords, and any specific elements to include (like CTAs or questions).

For Workflow and Project Setup (Chapters 10 & 11):

- **Structure (SOP Creation):** "*Help me create a Standard Operating Procedure (SOP) for [specific marketing task, e.g., 'onboarding a new client for social media management']. List all the key steps involved from initial contact to project kickoff. For each step, suggest key actions and any information to be collected or communicated.*"
- **Technique:** Focus on breaking down processes into logical steps. Ask the AI to think like a project manager or process analyst.

Advanced Prompting Techniques

Once you're comfortable with the basics, you can explore more advanced techniques:

- **Chain Prompting:** Using the output of one prompt as the input for the next. This is useful for complex tasks, allowing you to build upon previous results iteratively.
- **Zero-Shot Prompting:** Asking the AI to perform a task it hasn't been explicitly trained on with examples, relying on its general knowledge. This works best for simpler tasks or when you want a very novel output.

- **Role-Playing Scenarios:** Setting up a more elaborate scenario where the AI plays a specific character interacting with another (e.g., a customer service agent handling a complaint, or a sales representative pitching a product to a skeptical client). This can be great for generating dialogue or exploring different communication strategies.
- **Asking for Pros and Cons or Different Perspectives:** "*Discuss the pros and cons of using influencer marketing for a small e-commerce business.*" or "*Explain the concept of content marketing from the perspective of a customer versus the perspective of a business owner.*"
- **Requesting a Specific Output Structure (e.g., JSON, Markdown):** If you need the output in a particular structured format for use in other tools or for coding, you can often request it.
  - **Prompt Example:** "*Generate a list of 5 blog post ideas about sustainable living. Provide the output as a JSON array where each object has a 'title' and a 'brief_description' field.*"

Common Pitfalls to Avoid When Prompting

- **Being Too Vague:** "Tell me about marketing." (Too broad, will result in generic output).
- **Making Assumptions:** Assuming the AI knows your specific business context without providing it.
- **Overly Complex Single Prompts:** Trying to cram too many instructions or requests into one prompt can confuse the AI. Break it down.

- **Not Reviewing and Refining:** Accepting the AI's first output without critical review and editing.
- **Ignoring Tone and Audience:** Forgetting to specify the desired tone or consider the target audience for the content.
- **Ethical Blind Spots:** Asking the AI to generate misleading, harmful, or biased content. Always ensure your prompts and the resulting content adhere to ethical marketing practices.

Building Your Own Prompt Library

As you work more with your Agent, you'll discover prompts that consistently deliver great results for specific tasks. It's highly recommended to start building your own "prompt library" – a collection of your most effective prompts, categorized by task or marketing objective.

Your library could include:

- The exact prompt text.
- Notes on why it's effective.
- Examples of the output it generates.
- Variations you've tried.

This library will become an invaluable resource, saving you time and helping you maintain consistency in your AI-assisted marketing efforts. The Appendix of this book also contains a starter library of example prompts for various marketing tasks.

Practical Exercise: Refine a Prompt for a Specific Marketing Task

1. **Choose a Marketing Task:** Select a task you'd like your Agent to help with (e.g., writing a social media post, brainstorming ad copy, outlining a blog post).
2. **Write an Initial (Potentially Vague) Prompt:** Write a first attempt at a prompt for this task.
3. **Critique Your Prompt:** Using the principles discussed in this chapter, identify areas where your initial prompt could be clearer, more specific, or provide more context.
4. **Rewrite and Enhance Your Prompt:** Revise your prompt to incorporate more detail, define the desired output format, specify tone, add constraints, or even include an example.
5. **(Optional) Test Both Prompts:** If you can, test both your initial vague prompt and your revised, enhanced prompt with your Agent. Compare the quality of the outputs.
6. **Reflect on the Difference:** Note how the changes in your prompt affected the AI's response. This will help solidify your understanding of effective prompt engineering.

Pro-Tip: Experiment and Learn Continuously

The field of AI and prompt engineering is constantly evolving. Don't be afraid to experiment with different prompting styles and techniques. Pay attention to what works well for your specific needs and your Agent's capabilities. The more you practice, the more intuitive and effective your prompting will become, transforming your Agent into an even more powerful marketing partner.

CHAPTER 15

Your AI Agent for Efficiency: Saving Time and Money in Your Marketing Efforts

For any small business owner, two of the most constrained and valuable resources are undoubtedly time and money. Marketing, while essential for growth, can often feel like a significant drain on both. Throughout this book, we've explored how your Agent, Manus, can assist with a multitude of marketing tasks. This chapter focuses specifically on the tangible benefits of this partnership: how leveraging Manus can lead to substantial time savings and, consequently, cost reductions in your overall marketing operations. We will look at practical examples and scenarios to illustrate how AI-driven efficiency translates into a healthier bottom line and more bandwidth for you to focus on strategic growth. These tools are paid tools and a monthly fee may seem daunting at first but when you are able to explicitly see the savings and the benefits, the cost of the tools pales in comparison.

The True Cost of Marketing for Small Businesses

Before we discuss savings, it's important to acknowledge the typical costs associated with marketing for a small business, beyond just direct ad spend:

- **Time Investment:** Countless hours spent on research, content creation, social media management, email campaigns, website updates, and analyzing performance.
- **Opportunity Cost:** The time spent on routine marketing tasks is time *not* spent on core business operations, product development, customer service, or strategic planning.
- **Outsourcing Costs:** Many small businesses outsource specific marketing functions (e.g., content writing, SEO, social media management) to freelancers or agencies, which can be a significant expense.
- **Tool Subscriptions:** Costs for various marketing software (email marketing platforms, SEO tools, social media schedulers, design software).
- **Cost of Inefficiency:** Time wasted on ineffective strategies or poorly executed campaigns due to lack of expertise or bandwidth.

Your Agent can help mitigate many of these costs by empowering you to do more in-house, do it faster, and do it more effectively.

Quantifying Time Savings with Your AI Agent

While the exact time saved will vary depending on the task and your proficiency with prompting, here are key areas where Manus can dramatically reduce the hours you spend on marketing:

1. **Research and Information Gathering (Chapters 3 & 4):

- **Without AI:** Hours spent manually searching the web, sifting through articles, compiling competitor data, or trying to understand market trends.
- **With AI:** Manus can perform targeted research and summarize key findings in minutes. It can quickly identify competitor strategies or gather data for customer avatar creation, turning hours of work into a much shorter, focused session.
- *Potential Time Savings Example:* Researching 3 competitors used to take 4 hours. With Manus, gathering initial data and summaries might take 1 hour, allowing you to focus on analysis.

2. **Content Creation (Chapters 7, 8, 9, 10):

   - **Without AI:** Significant time spent brainstorming, outlining, drafting, and editing blog posts, website copy, social media updates, and emails.
   - **With AI:** Manus can generate outlines and first drafts rapidly. While you still need to edit and personalize, the initial heavy lifting is done, drastically cutting down creation time.
   - *Potential Time Savings Example:* Writing a 1000-word blog post from scratch might take 3-5 hours. With Manus drafting the initial content based on your outline, you might reduce this to 1-2 hours for review, editing, and adding your unique insights.

3. **Idea Generation and Brainstorming (Chapter 6):

   - **Without AI:** Creative blocks can lead to hours of unproductive thinking or expensive brainstorming sessions.

- **With AI:** Manus can act as an instant brainstorming partner, generating dozens of campaign ideas, content topics, or taglines in minutes, providing a wealth of starting points.
- *Potential Time Savings Example:* A 2-hour brainstorming meeting for a new campaign could be supplemented or even replaced by a 30-minute focused session with Manus to generate initial concepts.

4. **Repetitive Communication Tasks (Chapter 11):
   - **Without AI:** Manually drafting similar responses to frequently asked questions or crafting individual follow-up emails.
   - **With AI:** Manus can help create templates for common responses or draft personalized email sequences based on your criteria, saving time on routine communication.
5. **Basic SEO Tasks (Chapter 9):
   - **Without AI:** Time spent manually researching keyword ideas or trying to craft optimized meta descriptions from scratch.
   - **With AI:** Manus can quickly generate keyword suggestions or draft SEO-friendly titles and descriptions based on your content and target terms.

Translating Time Savings into Cost Reduction

The time you save by using your Agent directly translates into cost savings in several ways:

1. **Reduced Need for Outsourcing (or More Strategic Outsourcing):

   - If you were previously paying freelancers or agencies for tasks like content writing, basic SEO research, or social media content generation, Manus can help you bring more of this work in-house, significantly reducing these direct expenses.

   - Even if you continue to outsource, Manus can help you prepare better briefs, conduct initial research, or generate first drafts, potentially reducing the hours you pay for and allowing you to use outsourced experts for higher-level strategy and refinement.

   - *Cost Savings Example:* If you paid a content writer $100-$300 per blog post, and Manus helps you write 2-4 posts a month in-house, that's a direct saving of $200-$1200 per month.

2. **Increased Productivity (Doing More with the Same Resources):

   - The time saved allows you or your team to accomplish more marketing tasks within the same timeframe. This means you can expand your marketing efforts (e.g., post more frequently on social media, publish more blog content, run more targeted email campaigns) without increasing headcount or work hours.

   - This increased output can lead to faster growth, more leads, and ultimately more sales, all without a proportional increase in marketing labor costs.

3. **Lower Opportunity Costs:

   - By spending less time on routine marketing tasks, you free yourself up to focus on other critical business activities that directly generate revenue or improve operations, such as sales calls, product development, strategic partner-ships, or enhancing customer experiences.
   - The value of this reallocated time can be immense, far exceeding the direct cost of an Agent subscription (if applicable).

4. **Faster Speed to Market:

   - Manus can help you develop and launch marketing campaigns or new content much faster. This agility allows you to capitalize on emerging trends or respond quickly to market changes, potentially giving you a competitive edge and leading to quicker returns on marketing initiatives.

5. **Potential Reduction in Marketing Tool Overlap:

   - While Manus won't replace all specialized marketing tools, its versatility in areas like content generation, idea brainstorming, and basic research might reduce your reliance on multiple niche tools, potentially allowing you to consolidate your software subscriptions.

Scenarios: Illustrating Efficiency Gains

Scenario 1: The Solo Entrepreneur Launching a New Service

* **Challenge:** Needs to create website copy, a series of 5 introductory blog posts, a 3-email welcome sequence, and social media announcement posts, all with a very limited budget and time.

* **With Manus:** * Website copy (5 pages): Drafted with Manus in 4-6 hours (vs. 15-20 hours or $1000+ outsourced). * Blog posts (5): Outlined and drafted with Manus in 8-10 hours (vs. 20-25 hours or $500+ outsourced). * Email sequence (3 emails): Drafted with Manus in 2-3 hours (vs. 6-8 hours or $300+ outsourced). * Social media posts (10 posts): Drafted with Manus in 1-2 hours (vs. 4-5 hours).

* **Outcome:** Significant time saved, allowing for a faster launch. Direct cost savings by avoiding outsourcing for initial content creation.

Scenario 2: The Small Retail Business Wanting to Improve Local SEO

* **Challenge:** Needs to optimize their Google Business Profile, generate keyword ideas for local search, and create content for local landing pages.

* **With Manus:** * Google Business Profile: Business description, service descriptions, and FAQ answers drafted with Manus in 1-2 hours. * Local Keyword Research: Brainstormed 50+ local keyword ideas with Manus in 30 minutes. * Local Landing Page Copy (3 pages): Drafted with Manus in 3-4 hours.

* **Outcome:** Improved local visibility potentially leading to more foot traffic, achieved with minimal time investment and without needing to hire an expensive SEO consultant for these foundational tasks.

Maximizing Your ROI from Your AI Agent

To ensure you're getting the most significant time and cost savings from Manus:

- **Invest Time in Learning Effective Prompting (Chapter 12):** The better your prompts, the faster you'll get quality results, minimizing rework.
- **Identify Your Most Time-Consuming, Repetitive Tasks:** Prioritize using Manus for these areas first to see the quickest efficiency gains.
- **Integrate Manus into Your Existing Workflows (Chapter 10):** Don't treat it as a separate tool; make it a part of your regular marketing processes.
- **Continuously Experiment and Refine:** Explore different ways Manus can assist you and refine your approach based on what works best.
- **Remember the Human Element:** While Manus provides efficiency, your strategic oversight, brand knowledge, and personal touch are still crucial for final quality and impact.

Practical Exercise: Calculate Potential Time Savings for One Marketing Task

1. **Choose a Recurring Marketing Task:** Select a marketing task you perform regularly (e.g., writing a

weekly blog post, creating daily social media updates, researching monthly industry trends).

2. **Estimate Current Time Spent:** Honestly estimate how many hours you currently spend on this task each time you do it (or each week/month).
3. **Estimate Time with AI Assistance:** Based on what you've learned in this book, estimate how much time you think you could save by using your Agent to assist with the most time-consuming parts of that task (e.g., drafting, research).
4. **Calculate Potential Savings:** Subtract the estimated time with AI from the current time spent. Multiply this by how often you perform the task to see weekly or monthly time savings.
5. **(Optional) Assign a Monetary Value:** If you have an hourly rate for your time or know what it would cost to outsource that task, you can assign a monetary value to the time saved.

Pro-Tip: Reinvest Your Saved Time Wisely

The time and money saved through AI-driven efficiency are only valuable if reinvested wisely. Use this newfound bandwidth to focus on high-impact strategic activities, innovation, building deeper customer relationships, or even taking a well-deserved break to recharge your entrepreneurial batteries. Your Agent is there to make your marketing life easier and your business stronger, freeing you to be the visionary leader your small business needs.

CHAPTER 16

Leveraging Your AI Agent's Strengths: Data Analysis, Reporting, and Custom Tool Creation

As your familiarity with your Agent, Manus, grows, and new agents are introduces, you'll begin to see its potential extend beyond routine marketing tasks into more advanced applications. While Manus excels at research, content generation, and workflow assistance, its capabilities in processing information, understanding complex requests, and even generating code open doors to leveraging it for basic data analysis, report summarization, and even the conceptualization or rudimentary coding of simple custom marketing tools. This chapter explores these advanced use cases, demonstrating how Manus can become an even more integral part of your data-driven marketing strategy and innovation efforts.

Your Agent as a Data Interpretation Assistant

Small businesses today have access to a vast amount of marketing data from various sources: website analytics (Google Analytics), social media insights, email campaign reports, sales figures, and customer feedback. However, raw data is only useful if it can be interpreted to reveal actionable insights. While Manus is not a replacement for dedicated analytics platforms or a data scientist, it can assist you in making sense of data you provide to it.

Important Note: Manus does not directly access your private analytics dashboards or databases. You must provide the data to Manus in a text-based format (e.g., by copying and pasting tables, summarizing key metrics, or describing data patterns in your prompts).

How Manus Can Help with Data Analysis (When Data is Provided):

1. **Summarizing Key Metrics and Trends:** If you provide Manus with a set of performance metrics (e.g., website traffic sources over time, engagement rates for different social media post types, conversion rates for various ad campaigns), it can help you summarize the key takeaways or identify notable trends.

   – **Prompt Example**: "*I have the following website traffic data for the last 3 months: Month 1: Organic Search - 500 visits, Social Media - 200 visits, Direct - 100 visits. Month 2: Organic Search - 550 visits, Social Media - 250 visits, Direct - 120 visits. Month 3: Organic Search - 650 visits, Social Media - 230 visits, Direct - 110 visits. Summarize the key trends in traffic sources and overall growth.*"

2. **Identifying Patterns and Correlations (Conceptual):** By describing data sets, Manus can help you brainstorm potential correlations or patterns to investigate further. For instance, if you notice sales spiked after a particular marketing campaign and provide details of both, Manus could help you articulate the potential link.

3. **Interpreting Customer Feedback:** If you have a collection of customer reviews, survey responses, or social media comments, you can provide this text to Manus and ask it to identify common themes, sentiment (positive, negative, neutral), or frequently mentioned issues and praises.

   – **Prompt Example**: *"I've pasted 20 customer reviews for my product below [paste reviews]. Please analyze these reviews and identify the top 3 most frequently mentioned positive aspects and the top 2 most common complaints or areas for improvement."*

4. **Generating Hypotheses for A/B Testing:** Based on performance data you provide for different marketing variations (e.g., two different email subject lines), Manus can help you formulate hypotheses about why one performed better and suggest further tests.

Best Practices for Using Manus for Data Analysis:

- **Provide Clean, Structured Data:** The clearer and more organized the data you provide, the better Manus can assist.
- **Be Specific in Your Questions:** Ask targeted questions about the data rather than general requests.
- **Use Manus for Initial Insights, Not Definitive Analysis:** Manus can help you spot trends or summarize information, but for complex statistical analysis or business-critical decisions, rely on dedicated analytics tools and human expertise.
- **Verify Insights:** Always cross-reference insights generated by Manus with your own understanding and other data sources.

Generating Report Summaries and Outlines with Manus

Communicating marketing performance to stakeholders (even if it's just for your own strategic review) often involves creating reports. Manus can assist in drafting summaries or outlines for these reports based on the data and key messages you provide.

- **Creating Executive Summaries:** If you have a longer performance report or a collection of key metrics, Manus can help you draft a concise executive summary highlighting the most important achievements, challenges, and next steps.
- **Outlining Monthly or Quarterly Marketing Reports:** Manus can help you structure a marketing report, suggesting sections like "Key Performance Indicators (KPIs)," "Campaign Highlights," "Challenges and Learnings," and "Priorities for Next Period."
  - **Prompt Example**: "*Agent, help me outline a monthly marketing report for my e-commerce business. It should include sections for website traffic, sales conversions, email marketing performance, social media engagement, and key takeaways/actions for next month.*"

Conceptualizing and Assisting with Simple Custom Marketing Tools

One of the more advanced and exciting capabilities of Agents like Manus is their ability to understand and even generate code in various programming languages (like Python, JavaScript). While Manus won't build complex software applications for you, it can be surprisingly helpful in conceptualizing and even drafting code for simple custom marketing tools or scripts that can automate small tasks or provide specific calculations.

Disclaimer: You should have some basic understanding of coding concepts or work with a developer to implement and test any code generated by Manus. Always test code thoroughly in a safe environment before using it for critical tasks.

Examples of Simple Tools Manus Could Help Conceptualize or Draft Code For:

1. **Basic Marketing Calculators:**
   - A simple Return on Investment (ROI) calculator for marketing campaigns.
   - A Customer Lifetime Value (CLV) estimator (based on a formula you provide).
   - A break-even point calculator for a new product.
   - *Prompt Example (Conceptual): "I need a simple Python script that calculates marketing ROI. It should take 'Total Revenue from Campaign' and 'Total Cost of Campaign' as inputs and output the ROI as a percentage. Provide the formula used."*
2. **Text Manipulation Utilities:**
   - A script to count word frequency in a block of text (useful for analyzing customer feedback or content).
   - A tool to generate multiple variations of a headline by swapping out keywords.

3. **Simple Data Organization Scripts:**
   - If you have data in a simple text format (e.g., a list of customer email addresses with some tags), Manus can help you write a script to filter or sort that data based on criteria you define.
4. **Web Scrapers (Conceptual and Basic for Public Data):**
   - Manus might be able to help you outline the logic or even draft a very basic Python script (using libraries like BeautifulSoup or Scrapy, which you would need to install and run in your own environment) to extract publicly available information from a specific webpage (e.g., product names and prices from a competitor's site). **Always be mindful of website terms of service and ethical considerations when attempting any web scraping.**

The Process for Developing a Simple Tool with Manus:

1. **Clearly Define the Tool's Purpose:** What problem will it solve? What inputs will it take? What output should it produce?
2. **Outline the Logic:** Break down the steps the tool needs to perform.
3. **Prompt Manus for Code (Specify Language):** Ask Manus to generate the code, specifying the programming language (e.g., Python, JavaScript). Provide the logic and any formulas.

4. **Review and Understand the Code:** Even if you're not an expert coder, try to understand the basic structure of the code Manus provides.
5. **Test Thoroughly:** Test the code with various inputs in a safe development environment. Debug any errors (Manus can sometimes help with debugging if you provide the error messages and the relevant code snippet).
6. **Implement and Use (with Caution):** Once tested, you can use your simple custom tool.

Practical Exercise: Conceptualize a Simple Marketing Calculator

1. **Identify a Need:** Think of a simple calculation you frequently do for your marketing (e.g., calculating click-through rate, conversion rate from website visitors to leads, basic ad spend ROI).
2. **Define Inputs and Outputs:** What numbers do you start with? What number do you want to get?
3. **Write Down the Formula:** Clearly state the mathematical formula.
4. **Prompt Your Agent:** Ask your Agent to describe how it would create a simple script (e.g., in Python) to perform this calculation. You can even ask it to generate the code snippet.
   - **Example:** "*I want to calculate the click-through rate (CTR) for my emails. The formula is (Total Clicks / Total Emails Delivered)* 100. Can you generate a simple Python function that takes 'total_clicks'

and 'total_emails_ delivered' as input and returns the CTR as a percentage?*"

5. **Review the Concept/Code:** See if the AI's response makes sense and aligns with your understanding.

Pro-Tip: Start with Simple, Well-Defined Problems

When exploring custom tool creation with Manus, begin with very simple, clearly defined problems. As you gain confidence and understanding, you can gradually explore slightly more complex utilities. Remember that Manus is an assistant in this process; the strategic thinking, testing, and responsibility for implementation remain with you.

By tapping into these advanced capabilities, you can further enhance your marketing efficiency, gain deeper insights from your data, and even create bespoke solutions tailored to your unique business needs, making your Agent an even more indispensable partner in your growth journey.

CHAPTER 17

The Future of AI in Small Business Marketing and Your Agent's Role

As we conclude this journey through "Beyond GPT Smarter AI for Small Business Marketing," it's clear that Artificial Intelligence, and specifically Agents like Manus, are not just fleeting trends but foundational shifts in how businesses will operate and compete. The marketing landscape is in a perpetual state of evolution, and AI is currently one of its most powerful catalysts. For small businesses, this era presents both unprecedented opportunities and the challenge of adaptation. This final chapter will look ahead, exploring emerging trends in AI and marketing, discussing how your Agent is positioned to help you navigate this future, and encouraging a mindset of continuous learning and experimentation to ensure your business not only survives but thrives in the AI-powered age.

Emerging Trends in AI and Marketing: What to Watch For

The capabilities of AI are expanding at an astonishing rate. Here are some key trends that are likely to shape the future of marketing and how your Agent might play a role:

1. **Hyper-Personalization at Scale:**
   - **Trend:** AI will enable even deeper levels of personalization in marketing messages, product recommendations, and customer experiences, moving beyond segmentation to true one-to-one interaction at scale.
   - **Manus's Potential Role:** While Manus helps you understand your avatar now, future iterations or integrations might assist in analyzing vast customer datasets (with appropriate privacy safeguards) to identify micro-segments or individual preferences, helping you craft hyper-personalized campaign elements or content suggestions.
2. **Predictive Analytics for Proactive Marketing:**
   - **Trend:** AI algorithms will become increasingly adept at predicting customer behavior, identifying at-risk customers, forecasting sales trends, and optimizing marketing spend proactively.
   - **Manus's Potential Role:** Manus could assist in interpreting outputs from predictive analytics tools, helping you understand the implications and brainstorm strategic responses. It might also help in setting up conceptual models for simple predictive tasks based on data you provide.
3. **AI-Powered Content Generation Evolution:**
   - **Trend:** AI content generation will move beyond text to more sophisticated creation of images, video, and even interactive experiences, with increasing quality and realism.

- **Manus's Potential Role:** As AI multimedia generation tools become more accessible, Manus could act as a central interface for prompting and orchestrating the creation of diverse content assets, ensuring brand consistency across different formats.

4. **Conversational AI and Advanced Chatbots:**
   - **Trend:** AI-powered chatbots and virtual assistants will become more human-like, capable of handling complex customer service inquiries, providing personalized shopping assistance, and even engaging in nuanced sales conversations.
   - **Manus's Potential Role:** Manus can already help you draft responses and FAQs. In the future, it might assist in designing more complex conversational flows for chatbots or even integrate more directly with such platforms (depending on its development path).
5. **AI in Voice Search and Auditory Experiences:**
   - **Trend:** With the rise of smart speakers and voice assistants, optimizing for voice search and creating branded auditory experiences (like podcast snippets or audio ads) will become more important.
   - **Manus's Potential Role:** Manus can help you research voice search keywords, brainstorm ideas for audio content, and draft scripts optimized for spoken delivery.

6. **Ethical AI and Data Privacy Focus:**
   - **Trend:** As AI becomes more powerful, there will be an increasing focus on ethical considerations, data privacy, algorithmic bias, and transparency in how AI is used in marketing.
   - **Manus's Potential Role:** Manus can help you research best practices for ethical AI use and data privacy regulations, ensuring your marketing efforts remain responsible and trustworthy. It can also be a tool to help you articulate your own data privacy policies.
7. **AI for Enhanced Customer Journey Mapping:**
   - **Trend:** AI will provide deeper insights into complex customer journeys across multiple touchpoints, helping businesses optimize each stage for better conversion and retention.
   - **Manus's Potential Role:** By helping you analyze customer feedback and interaction data (that you provide), Manus can assist in identifying pain points and opportunities within your current customer journey, and brainstorm ways to improve it.

Your Agent: A Partner for Future Success

Your Agent, Manus, is designed to be an adaptable and evolving partner. As AI technology advances, Manus will likely gain new capabilities and become even more adept at assisting you with these emerging marketing trends. The key is to view Manus not as a static tool but as a dynamic collaborator that can grow with your business.

Here's how Manus is positioned to help you navigate the future:

- **Continuous Learning (for You and the AI):** The more you interact with Manus, providing feedback and clear instructions, the better it understands your specific needs and preferences. Simultaneously, you will become more skilled at leveraging its capabilities.
- **Adaptability:** Agents are built to process and understand new information. As new marketing strategies or technologies emerge, you can use Manus to research them, understand their implications, and brainstorm how to adapt your business.
- **Efficiency and Scalability:** As your business grows, Manus can help you scale your marketing efforts without a proportional increase in manual labor, handling more research, content generation, and workflow assistance.
- **Democratization of Advanced Capabilities:** Agents like Manus make sophisticated marketing assistance more accessible to small businesses that may not have the resources for large in-house teams or expensive specialized agencies.

Cultivating a Mindset of Continuous Learning and Experimentation

The most crucial factor for thriving in the AI-powered future of marketing is your mindset. Embrace a spirit of:

- **Curiosity:** Stay curious about new AI tools, marketing techniques, and shifts in consumer behavior. Use Manus to explore these topics.

- **Experimentation:** Don't be afraid to try new things. Use Manus to help you brainstorm and implement small marketing experiments. Analyze the results (with Manus's assistance if needed) and learn from both successes and failures.
- **Adaptability:** Be prepared to change your strategies and processes as the landscape evolves. What works today might not work tomorrow.
- **Lifelong Learning:** The world of AI and digital marketing is not static. Commit to ongoing learning to keep your skills and knowledge current.
- **Ethical Responsibility:** Always consider the ethical implications of using AI in your marketing. Prioritize transparency, fairness, and respect for customer privacy.

The Human Element Remains Irreplaceable

While AI offers incredible power and efficiency, it's vital to remember that the human element in marketing remains irreplaceable. Your creativity, empathy, strategic thinking, brand passion, and ability to build genuine relationships with your customers are qualities that AI can augment but not replicate.

Use Manus to handle the repetitive, data-intensive, and time-consuming aspects of marketing, freeing yourself to focus on:

- **High-Level Strategy:** Defining your brand vision, setting marketing goals, and making key strategic decisions.

- **Deep Customer Understanding:** Going beyond data to truly understand the emotional needs and motivations of your customers.
- **Creative Inspiration and Originality:** Using AI-generated ideas as a starting point, but infusing them with your unique creative spark.
- **Building Authentic Relationships:** Engaging with your customers on a personal level, fostering community, and providing exceptional human-to-human service.
- **Ethical Oversight:** Ensuring your marketing practices are responsible and aligned with your brand values.

A Final Word: Your Journey with AI Marketing

Mastering your Agent for marketing is not a one-time achievement but an ongoing journey. The tools will evolve, new strategies will emerge, and your business will grow and change. By embracing the principles outlined in this book – clear communication with your AI, strategic thinking, continuous learning, and a commitment to ethical practices – you are well-equipped to navigate this exciting future.

Your Agent is more than just software; it's a partner that can help you unlock new levels of creativity, efficiency, and growth for your small business. Embrace the collaboration, stay curious, and confidently step into the future of marketing, knowing you have a powerful ally by your side. The potential is limitless, and the journey has just begun.

NOTE TO READERS

Beyond the Book: Expert Implementation Available

While this book equips you with all the knowledge to create powerful AI marketing reports, we understand that time is your most valuable asset. For business owners focused on growth rather than implementation:

Right On Time Marketing Reports

We can create any of the reports described in this book specifically for your business.

- Market Opportunity Analysis - Identify untapped niches
- Ideal Customer Profile - Your most profitable customers
- Competitor Landscape Report - Strengths and weaknesses
- Product-Market Fit Assessment - Match offerings to needs
- Brand Messaging Guide - Core value propositions

Scan this QR code to learn more about how we can help you focus on running your business while we handle the marketing intelligence reports.

Appendices

CURRENTLY THIS IS THE BEST ONGOING TRAINING COURSE ON MANUS THAT I RECOMMEND

Appendix A: Glossary of Terms

This glossary provides definitions for key AI and marketing terms used throughout this book. Understanding this terminology will help you better comprehend the concepts discussed and communicate more effectively about your marketing strategies.

- **A/B Testing (Split Testing):** A method of comparing two versions of a webpage, email, or advertisement against each other to determine which one performs better. For example, testing two different headlines for an email to see which gets a higher open rate.
- **Agent (Artificial Intelligence Agent):** A software entity that perceives its environment through sensors and acts upon that environment through actuators. In the context of this book, Manus is your Agent, designed to assist with various tasks through intelligent interaction.
- **Algorithm:** A set of rules or instructions given to an AI, computer, or other problem-solving machine to help it calculate or solve a problem.
- **Alt Text (Alternative Text):** A textual description of an image on a webpage. It serves to describe the image to visually impaired users (via screen readers) and to search engines, aiding in image SEO.
- **Analytics:** The discovery, interpretation, and communication of meaningful patterns in data. In marketing, this involves tracking and analyzing data from websites, social media, email campaigns, etc., to measure performance and inform strategy.

- **API (Application Programming Interface):** A set of rules and protocols that allows different software applications to communicate and exchange data with each other.
- **Avatar (Customer Avatar/Persona):** A semi-fictional, detailed profile of your ideal customer, based on market research and real data about your existing customers. It helps you understand your target audience on a deeper level.
- **B2B (Business-to-Business):** Describes companies that sell products or services primarily to other businesses.
- **B2C (Business-to-Consumer):** Describes companies that sell products or services directly to individual consumers.
- **Blog:** A regularly updated website or web page, typically one run by an individual or small group, that is written in an informal or conversational style. Used in marketing for content creation, SEO, and audience engagement.
- **Brand Awareness:** The extent to which consumers are familiar with the distinctive qualities or image of a particular brand of goods or services.
- **Brand Voice:** The distinct personality a brand takes on in its communications. It encompasses the tone, language, and style used to connect with the audience.
- **Call to Action (CTA):** An instruction to the audience designed to provoke an immediate response, usually using an imperative verb such as "Call now," "Find out more," or "Visit our website."

- **Chatbot:** A computer program designed to simulate human conversation through voice or text commands, often used for customer service or lead generation.
- **Click-Through Rate (CTR):** The percentage of people who see an online ad or email and then click on it. Calculated as (Total Clicks / Total Impressions or Emails Delivered) * 100.
- **Content Management System (CMS):** A software application that allows users to create, manage, and modify content on a website without the need for specialized technical knowledge (e.g., WordPress, Shopify, Squarespace).
- **Content Marketing:** A strategic marketing approach focused on creating and distributing valuable, relevant, and consistent content to attract and retain a clearly defined audience — and, ultimately, to drive profitable customer action.
- **Conversion Rate:** The percentage of users or visitors who complete a desired action (a "conversion"), such as making a purchase, filling out a form, or signing up for a newsletter.
- **Crawling (Web Crawling):** The process by which search engine bots (crawlers or spiders) systematically browse the internet to discover and index web pages.
- **Customer Journey:** The complete sum of experiences that customers go through when interacting with your company and brand. Instead of looking at just a part of a transaction or experience, the customer journey documents the full experience of being a customer.

- **Customer Lifetime Value (CLV):** A prediction of the net profit attributed to the entire future relationship with a customer.
- **Data Analysis:** The process of inspecting, cleansing, transforming, and modeling data with the goal of discovering useful information, informing conclusions, and supporting decision-making.
- **Demographics:** Statistical data relating to the population and particular groups within it, such as age, gender, income, education, and occupation.
- **Email Marketing:** A form of direct marketing that uses email to promote a business's products or services. It can also be used to build relationships with potential customers or clients.
- **Engagement Rate:** A metric used to measure the level of interaction that content receives from an audience. It can include likes, shares, comments, clicks, etc., relative to reach or impressions.
- **FAQ (Frequently Asked Questions):** A list of common questions asked by customers, along with their answers, typically found on a website.
- **Few-Shot Prompting:** An AI prompting technique where you provide the AI with a few examples of the desired input-output behavior to guide its response for a new input.
- **Google Business Profile (GBP):** A free tool from Google that allows businesses to manage their online presence across Google, including Search and Maps.

- **Hashtag:** A word or phrase preceded by a hash sign (#), used on social media websites and applications to identify messages on a specific topic.
- **Header Tags (H1-H6):** HTML tags used to define headings and subheadings on a webpage, helping to structure content and signal importance to search engines.
- **Impressions:** The number of times a piece of content (like an ad or a social media post) is displayed, whether or not it is clicked on.
- **Indexing (Search Engine Indexing):** The process by which search engines organize the information they've gathered during crawling into a large database (index) so that it can be quickly retrieved during a search query.
- **Internal Linking:** The practice of linking from one page on your website to another page on your own website.
- **Keyword:** A specific word or phrase that describes the content of a webpage or an ad. Keywords are what users type into search engines.
- **Keyword Research:** The process of finding and analyzing the search terms that people enter into search engines with the goal of using that data for a specific purpose, often for search engine optimization (SEO) or general marketing.
- **Landing Page:** A standalone web page, created specifically for a marketing or advertising campaign. It's where a visitor "lands" after they click on a link in an email, or ads from Google, Bing, YouTube,

Facebook, Instagram, Twitter, or similar places on the web.

- **Lead Generation:** The marketing process of stimulating and capturing interest in a product or service for the purpose of developing a sales pipeline.
- **Lead Nurturing:** The process of developing and reinforcing relationships with buyers at every stage of the sales funnel.
- **Local SEO:** The process of optimizing your online presence to attract more business from relevant local searches, particularly for businesses with a physical location or service area.
- **Long-Tail Keywords:** Longer, more specific keyword phrases that visitors are more likely to use when they're closer to a point-of-purchase or when they're using voice search.
- **Machine Learning (ML):** A subset of artificial intelligence (AI) that provides systems the ability to automatically learn and improve from experience without being explicitly programmed.
- **Meta Description:** An HTML attribute that provides a brief summary of a webpage. It is often displayed in search engine results below the title tag.
- **NAP (Name, Address, Phone number):** Critical business information that needs to be consistent across all online listings for Local SEO.
- **Natural Language Processing (NLP):** A branch of artificial intelligence that helps computers understand, interpret, and manipulate human language.

- **On-Page SEO:** The practice of optimizing individual web pages in order to rank higher and earn more relevant traffic in search engines. It refers to both the content and HTML source code of a page.
- **Organic Traffic:** Visitors who come to your website from unpaid search engine results.
- **Prompt (AI Prompt):** The input (text, question, instruction) given to an AI model to elicit a specific response or generate desired output.
- **Prompt Engineering:** The process of structuring text that can be interpreted and understood by a generative AI model. It involves designing, refining, and optimizing prompts to get the best possible output from the AI.
- **Psychographics:** The study and classification of people according to their attitudes, aspirations, and other psychological criteria, especially in market research.
- **Reach:** The total number of unique people who see your content.
- **Return on Investment (ROI):** A performance measure used to evaluate the efficiency or profitability of an investment or compare the efficiency of a number of different investments. Marketing ROI = (Net Profit from Marketing / Cost of Marketing) * 100.
- **Search Engine Optimization (SEO):** The process of improving the quality and quantity of website traffic to a website or a web page from search engines. SEO

targets unpaid traffic (known as "natural" or "organic" results) rather than direct traffic or paid traffic.

- **Search Engine Results Page (SERP):** The page displayed by a web search engine in response to a query by a searcher.
- **Seed Keywords:** Broad, foundational terms related to your business or industry that are used as a starting point for more detailed keyword research.
- **Sentiment Analysis:** The process of computationally identifying and categorizing opinions expressed in a piece of text, especially in order to determine whether the writer's attitude towards a particular topic, product, etc., is positive, negative, or neutral.
- **Sitemap:** A file where you provide information about the pages, videos, and other files on your site, and the relationships between them. Search engines like Google read this file to more intelligently crawl your site.
- **Social Media Marketing (SMM):** The use of social media platforms and websites to promote a product or service.
- **Standard Operating Procedure (SOP):** A set of step-by-step instructions compiled by an organization to help workers carry out complex routine operations.
- **SWOT Analysis:** A strategic planning technique used to help a person or organization identify Strengths, Weaknesses, Opportunities, and Threats related to business competition or project planning.
- **Target Audience:** A particular group of consumers at which a product or service is aimed.

- **Title Tag:** An HTML element that specifies the title of a web page. Title tags are displayed on search engine results pages (SERPs) as the clickable headline for a given result, and are important for usability, SEO, and social sharing.
- **Unique Selling Proposition (USP):** The factor or consideration presented by a seller as the reason that one product or service is different from and better than that of the competition.
- **User Experience (UX):** The overall experience a person has when using a product, such as a website or computer application, especially in terms of how easy or pleasing it is to use.
- **Workflow Automation:** The design, execution, and automation of processes based on workflow rules where human tasks, data, or files are routed between people or systems based on pre-defined business rules.
- **Zero-Shot Prompting:** An AI prompting technique where the AI is asked to perform a task it hasn't been explicitly trained on with examples, relying on its general knowledge.

Appendix B: Resource List

This list provides a curated starting point for tools, platforms, and educational resources that complement your work with AI agents like Manus. These resources support content creation, research, automation, email marketing, SEO, and strategic implementation. (Note: The AI landscape evolves rapidly—visit tool websites directly to confirm current features and offerings.)

AI & Marketing News + Strategy Blogs

Marketing AI Institute – News, education, and tools for marketers using artificial intelligence.

Ben's Bites – A fast, daily newsletter highlighting the latest AI tools, trends, and case studies.

HubSpot Blog – Widely respected marketing blog with a growing focus on AI and automation.

Content Marketing Institute – Frameworks, guides, and insights on content strategy, many now integrating AI tools.

Search Engine Journal – Practical updates and expert commentary on SEO, AI search behavior, and marketing tech.

TechCrunch (AI section) – Covers startup news, funding rounds, and innovation in AI tools and infrastructure.

AI-Powered SEO & Research Tools

Google Keyword Planner – Free keyword research tool available through Google Ads.

Google Analytics 4 (GA4) – Website performance tracking with machine learning-powered insights.

Google Search Console – Essential for monitoring site indexing, performance, and keyword visibility.

Ahrefs – Paid SEO platform with site auditing, keyword analysis, and competitor research tools.

Semrush – All-in-one marketing suite offering AI-enhanced SEO and content marketing tools.

Moz Pro – A trusted suite of SEO tools with keyword tracking, site auditing, and link research.

Surfer SEO – AI-integrated content optimization tool that guides real-time on-page SEO improvements.

NeuronWriter – SEO editor using natural language processing to align content with search intent.

Content Creation & Visual Tools

Grammarly – AI-enhanced writing assistant for grammar, clarity, tone, and conciseness.

Canva – Graphic design platform with AI-generated templates and design suggestions.

Syllaby – AI platform for generating short-form video scripts, content calendars, and social-ready posts.

Descript – Audio and video editing platform with transcription, screen recording, and AI voice tools.

Social Media Scheduling & Automation

Hootsuite – Social media management platform with publishing, scheduling, and performance tracking.

Later – A visual social media planner for Instagram, TikTok, and Pinterest with built-in optimization tools.

Ocoya – Combines scheduling, AI copywriting, and graphic templates in one platform.

Email Marketing Platforms

beehiiv – Newsletter platform optimized for growth, monetization, and segmentation.

Mailchimp – A solid starting point for beginners, offering templates, autoresponders, and basic automations.

Customer Relationship Management (CRM)

HighLevel (GHL) – Full-service CRM with funnels, landing pages, automations, SMS/email outreach, and client pipeline management.

AI for Personal Research & Knowledge Management

Notebook LM – AI tool by Google that allows users to interact with their own documents through natural language queries.

Rewind AI – Records and stores everything seen or said on your device, making your digital experience fully searchable.

Mem AI – AI-powered note-taking tool that connects, organizes, and recalls information contextually.

AI for Project & Workflow Management

Taskade AI – Collaborative productivity tool with AI agents, mind maps, and structured workflows.

MindPal – An emerging platform to run and coordinate multiple AI agents across research and business tasks.

AI-Powered Customer Interaction

Tidio AI – Live chat and chatbot platform powered by conversational AI for e-commerce and lead generation.

ZipChat AI – No-code chatbot builder trained on your website content and powered by GPT-based models.

Learning Prompt Engineering

LearnPrompting.org – Free, open-source resource for mastering prompt writing and structure.

PromptHero – Searchable prompt gallery for visual and text-based AI applications.

OpenAI Cookbook – Technical resource and prompt-writing guide hosted on GitHub.

Claude Docs (Anthropic) – Documentation and best practices for using Claude AI effectively.

Ethical AI & Data Privacy Resources

Future of Privacy Forum (FPF) – A nonprofit focused on responsible data use and ethical AI deployment.

Information Commissioner's Office (ICO – UK) – Regulatory guidance on data protection, AI transparency, and consumer rights.

AI Incident Database – Real-world database of notable AI misuse, bias, and deployment failures for learning and accountability.

OECD AI Principles – Internationally recognized guidelines for safe, transparent, and trustworthy AI.

Appendix C: Example Prompts Library

This library provides a categorized collection of example prompts that you can adapt and use with your Agent for various marketing tasks discussed in this book. Remember to replace bracketed placeholders [like this] with your specific information.

Market Research & Avatar Development

(Chapter 2):

Here is an example of how to reference your knowledge base in a prompt:

"I'm working on a new email campaign for our premium skincare line. Please reference our brand voice guidelines that I've added to our knowledge base named [name of knowledge base]. Based on our previous email campaign performance metrics that I've also included in the knowledge base, help me draft an email announcement for our new anti-aging serum that's consistent with our brand voice and incorporates what we've learned from our previous campaigns."

Creating a System of Specialized AI Approaches

Content Creation Approach

- Example prompt: "*You are my content creation assistant. Please follow our brand voice guidelines that emphasize a friendly, educational tone with no technical jargon. Use our standard blog post structure with a compelling question as the headline, personal story in the introduction, three main points with subheadings, and an action-oriented conclusion. I need a blog post about [topic].*"

Research Approach

- Example prompt: *"You are my research assistant. When analyzing competitors, please evaluate their pricing strategy, unique selling proposition, content approach, and customer sentiment. Present findings in our standard competitive analysis format with strengths, weaknesses, opportunities, and threats clearly identified. I need research on [competitor/ topic]."*

Customer Service Approach

- Example prompt: "You are my customer service assistant. When drafting responses to customer inquiries, please maintain our empathetic but efficient tone, acknowledge the customer's concern specifically, provide a clear solution, and end with our standard closing that invites further questions if needed. Help me respond to this customer inquiry: [inquiry]."

Analytics Approach

- Example prompt: *"You are my analytics assistant. When reviewing campaign performance, please compare against our historical benchmarks, identify the top three factors influencing results, and provide specific, actionable recommendations for improvement based on the data. Analyze these campaign results: [data]."*

(Chapters 3 & 4):

- **Identify Market Trends:**
  - *"Research and summarize the top 3 emerging consumer trends in the [e.g., 'sustainable home goods'] market for [current year]. Focus on purchasing drivers and concerns. Cite sources if available."*

- **Competitor Analysis (Overview):**
  - *"Identify the top 3 direct competitors for a small business offering [e.g., 'online fitness coaching for busy moms'] in [e.g., 'the United States']. For each, briefly describe their main services and apparent target audience."*
- **Competitor Marketing Analysis (Specific):**
  - *"Analyze the website content and Instagram presence of [competitor website URL or name]. What are their primary marketing messages, content themes, and calls to action? What is their brand voice like?"*
- **SWOT Analysis Data Gathering:**
  - *"Based on public information, what are some potential strengths and weaknesses of [competitor name] in the [industry] market? What are some general opportunities and threats in this market currently?"*
- **Customer Avatar - Pain Points Research:**
  - *"Search online forums (like Reddit r/[relevant_subreddit] or Quora) and social media discussions related to [e.g., 'learning a new language as an adult']. What are the most common frustrations, challenges, and desired outcomes people express?"*
- **Draft Customer Avatar Profile:**
  - *"Based on the following insights: [paste summary of research: e.g., target audience is 30-45, interested in career advancement, struggles with finding time, values practical learning], draft a customer avatar profile for an online course on [e.g., 'Business English']. Name the avatar 'Ambitious Alex.' Include sections for Demographics, Goals, Challenges, Values, and Information Sources."*

Idea Generation & Creativity (Chapter 6):

- **Marketing Campaign Ideas:**
  - *"I run a [e.g., 'local independent bookstore']. Brainstorm 7 unique marketing campaign ideas for [e.g., 'Independent Bookstore Day'] that would encourage foot traffic and community engagement. Keep ideas budget-friendly."*

- **Blog Post Titles:**
  - *"My business sells [e.g., 'artisanal dog treats']. Generate 15 engaging blog post titles that would appeal to dog owners interested in healthy pet food and training tips."*
- **Tagline Generation:**
  - *"Generate 10 catchy taglines for a new [e.g., 'eco-friendly subscription box service']. The brand voice is [e.g., 'uplifting and conscious']."*
- **USP Brainstorming:**
  - *"Help me brainstorm potential Unique Selling Propositions (USPs) for my [e.g., 'custom software development service for startups']. Key differentiators are [e.g., 'rapid prototyping, transparent pricing, dedicated project managers']. My target avatar is a non-technical startup founder."*

Content Creation (Chapters 7, 8, 9, 10):

- **Website Homepage Copy Outline:**
  - *"Outline the key sections for the homepage copy of a website for a [e.g., 'personal chef service']. The goal is to attract busy professionals looking for healthy meal solutions. Include a strong headline idea, an introduction,*

sections for 'How it Works,' 'Benefits,' 'Testimonial Snippet Placeholder,' and a primary Call to Action."

- **Blog Post Draft (from outline):**
  - *"Act as an expert in [topic, e.g., 'sustainable gardening']. Write a first draft (approx. 800 words) for a blog post based on the following outline: [paste your outline]. The tone should be informative and encouraging for beginners. Incorporate the keyword '[primary keyword]' 3-5 times naturally."*
- **Email Subject Line Options:**
  - *"Generate 5 compelling email subject lines for a promotional email announcing a [e.g., '20% off sale on all summer dresses']. Aim for a sense of urgency and curiosity."*
- **Social Media Caption (Instagram):**
  - *"Write an engaging Instagram caption (around 100 words) for an image showing [e.g., 'a beautifully plated dish from our new menu']. The tone should be [e.g., 'mouth-watering and sophisticated']. Include 3 relevant food hashtags and a question to encourage engagement."*
- **Video Script Outline:**
  - *"Create a script outline for a 1-minute explainer video about our [e.g., 'new mobile app for budget tracking']. It should cover: 1. The problem (difficulty managing finances). 2. Our app as the solution. 3. Top 3 features/ benefits. 4. Call to action (download the app). Suggest simple visuals for each section."*
- **Meta Description:**

- *"Write a compelling meta description (under 155 characters) for a webpage about [e.g., 'our handcrafted leather bags']. Include the keyword '[e.g., handmade leather bags]' and a benefit for the user."*

Workflow, Setup, and Efficiency (Chapters 11, 12, 14):

- **SOP Outline:**
  - *"Help me outline a Standard Operating Procedure (SOP) for [e.g., 'responding to customer inquiries on social media']. Include steps for monitoring, initial response time goals, common inquiry types, escalation procedures, and tone of voice guidelines."*
- **Brainstorming Repetitive Tasks for AI Assistance:**
  - *"I spend a lot of time on [e.g., 'manually creating weekly social media reports by copying data from platform insights']. What are some ways an AI assistant could conceptually help streamline parts of this process, assuming I can provide the data in text format?"*

Advanced Prompts (Chapter 13 & 15):

- **Assigning a Persona:**
  - *"Act as a skeptical small business owner who is hesitant about using AI for marketing. Ask me three challenging questions about the real benefits and potential downsides."*
- **Few-Shot Prompting (Example-Led):**

– *"I need short, benefit-driven descriptions for online courses. Example 1: 'Course: Excel for Beginners. Master spreadsheets and boost your job skills in just 4 weeks.' Example 2: 'Course: Mindful Meditation. Reduce stress and find calm in your daily life.' Now, write a similar description for: 'Course: Introduction to Python Programming.'"*

- **Requesting Structured Output (JSON):**
  – *"Generate a list of 3 potential names for a new coffee shop. Provide the output as a JSON array of strings."*
- **Data Interpretation (from provided text):**
  – *"I have pasted customer survey feedback below regarding our new software feature [paste feedback text]. Please summarize the top 3 positive comments and the top 3 areas of concern or confusion mentioned by users."*

Remember to adapt these examples to your specific business, target audience, and the unique capabilities of your Agent. The key is to be clear, provide context, and iterate!

DOWNLOAD THE RESOURCE GUIDE WITH ALL THE PROMPTS AND THE APPENDICES

Made in the USA
Monee, IL
04 November 2026

67387467R10105